Russian Supply Efforts in America During the First World War

Russian Supply Efforts in America During the First World War

Dale C. Rielage

McFarland & Company, Inc., Publishers
Jefferson, North Carolina, and London

Library of Congress Cataloguing-in-Publication Data

Rielage, Dale C., 1970–
Russian supply efforts in America during the First World War / Dale C. Rielage.
p. cm.
Includes bibliographical references and index.

ISBN 0-7864-1337-9 (softcover binding : 50# alkaline paper) ∞

1. World War, 1914–1918—Equipment and supplies. 2. World War, 1914–1918—Transportation. 3. World War, 1914–1918—Russia. 4. United States—Foreign relations—Russia. 5. Russia—Foreign relations—United States. I. Title.
D639.S9R54 2002
940.4'1028—dc21 2002007199

British Library cataloguing data are available

Cover photograph: The United States transport ship *Crooks* unloading supplies in Vladivostok in 1918 *(U.S. Official Pictures of the War, ©1920)*

Manufactured in the United States of America

McFarland & Company, Inc., Publishers
Box 611, Jefferson, North Carolina 28640
www.mcfarlandpub.com

Acknowledgments

This project was born from a single footnote in Lewis H. Siegelbaum's outstanding work *The Politics of Industrial Mobilization in Russia: A Study of the War-Industries Committees*. With the encouragement of Austin Jersild, this brief reference to the War-Industries Committee representative in the United States during World War I became my point of departure for the multi-year adventure that ultimately became this work.

That the shortcomings this work has are mine alone should be self-evident. What virtues it has are due to the assistance of a number of patient and thoughtful persons. I owe particular thanks to Carl Boyd and Craig Cameron of the history department at Old Dominion University, who served as readers for the original project and provided the exacting and insightful comments that are their trademarks. Thomas T. Taber, administrator of the Railroad Historical Research Center, provided insight into the U.S. locomotive industry around World War I and offered useful comments on Chapter 5.

A number of long-suffering research librarians went beyond the call to find particularly obscure and difficult sources. I owe a special debt to the library staff at Old Dominion University, the Joint Forces Staff College library, especially Marie Harrison, and the staff at the Albert H. Small Special Collections Library at the University of Virginia.

Finally and most importantly, my thanks to my wife, Lisa, the ideal research assistant, sounding board and friend.

Contents

Acknowledgments v

Introduction 1

1—The Early War Orders 11

2—The Crisis Breaks 33

3—A Committee in Earnest 47

4—The Russian-British Axis Cemented 63

5—The Zemsky Buy a Railroad: A Case Study 75

6—The Liberals in Control 87

7—Bolshevik Revolution and Closure 99

8—Conclusion 109

Appendix A—Chronology of Events Relating to Russian Supply with Major Wartime Events 113

Appendix B—Procedure to Be Pursued for the Purchase of Machine Tools for Russia in America 117

Appendix C—Statute Governing the Russian Supply Committee in America 119
Appendix D—Agreement Establishing the Anglo-Russian Sub-Committee 125

Notes 129
Bibliography 153
Index 161

Introduction

The Tsarist government between 1914 and 1917 failed to meet its wartime needs despite great effort to purchase military supplies in America. This is the story of that purchasing effort, the contracts it secured and the supplies it did not.

Supplying Russia's armies was a task of clear national importance, and purchasing on the American market enlisted not only official government agencies but activist non-governmental organizations representing Russian civil society. The Tsarist bureaucracy, both civil and military, proved unable to transcend internal differences to create a unified and effective purchasing process. Russian civil society, cognizant of government failures, pursued its own orders, further disrupting purchasing efforts in America and hampering the war effort it sought to assist. Both groups ultimately proved unable to adapt to the unfamiliar arena of the American market.

On immediate inspection, the collection of institutions and ideas that define late Imperial Russia comprise a textbook example of a society failing to adapt to change. In the popular mind, the Russian regime, like its Austro-Hungarian counterpart, was an expression of a different era, poised to be swept away by the tides of history. Against this simplistic explanation, apologists for the regime, beginning with pro-Tsarist Russian exiles, have offered the argument that change was possible within the Tsarist system. The pre-war Tsarist government produced at least two innovative ministers, Serge Witte and Peter Stolypin, who provide evidence that the government, despite its general inefficiency and reaction, did produce a number of gifted politicians and administrators. Leaders of industrial and agricultural policy evinced the willingness to make difficult choices and, often with a measure of political and social pain, to reform critical sectors of Russian society. Representatives of the failed Russian government later argued that, without the unplanned strains of the First World War, the government could eventually have found a less catastrophic route to reform.

Those who believe that the gradual reform of Russian society was possible more commonly place their faith in the nascent elements of Tsarist civil society. Despite the essentially autocratic nature of the Tsarist government, elements of civil society were present in late Tsarist Russia and were gradually increasing in both their size and scope of action. In the liberal view, these organs could ultimately have brought Russia to some form of constitutional government. The coming of the First World War prevented this natural development. Further, Russian liberals held that responsibility for the underdevelopment of the organs of civil society and the failures these groups experienced while addressing social problems could be blamed on the Tsarist state.

This positive view of Russian civil society has been influential in the United States and Western Europe since well before 1917. Prominent members of Russian liberal society were cosmopolitan in outlook and had well-developed ties to the United States and Britain.[1] In a real sense, western elites saw Russian liberals as their counterparts in Russian society and took comfort in the idea that Russia's progress would, in time, be guided by people "just like us." After the fall of the Provisional Government, these liberals defined the Russian revolution for foreign audiences. For their former allies, they became the interpreters of the early Soviet regime, apologists for the Provisional Government and advocates for the Whites. Once Soviet power was established, they remained in the West, writing their memoirs and forming the nucleus of Russian studies programs in academia. Their view of the prospects of civil society, however, was defined by their role in those very organs. Accomplished and Western-oriented, these Russian émigrés created the texts that became the West's master narrative of events in Revolutionary Russia.[2]

In recent years, an increasing body of literature has grown around questions of civil society in late Imperial Russia. As Theodore Von Laue observed, it is difficult to assess the prospects for the Imperial government or Russian liberalism when the Bolsheviks so convincingly disposed of both.[3] Several of these works have attempted to contrast government and social efforts to address a common problem. Such a case study approach offers the opportunity to contrast methods and effectiveness, as well as interactions between the two groups. Ideally a case study would involve compelling interests that would encourage cooperation. It would also address a problem that was presented to both elements simultaneously, rather than the more common movement of Russian civil society into areas of governmental concern.

Imperial Russian efforts during the First World War to secure military supplies from overseas producers, particularly the United States, provide such an opportunity for study. At various points during the war, representatives of both Tsarist bureaucracy and civil society participated in securing and administering the purchase of overseas supplies. The question of adaptability to change is a key issue in judging whether either group possessed the ability to answer the challenges of a changing Russia. The military supply situation between 1914 and 1917 was something new and unforeseen in Russian and international circles. While the Russian state had domestic mechanisms for military supply and had, on occasion, purchased arms abroad, the permanent foreign dependence beginning in early 1915 was fundamentally new. With no bureaucracy in place to answer this need, the Russian government's efforts are indicative of official response to new situations.

The question of overseas supplies also provides a basis for comparison between nations. None of the belligerent powers entered the First World War prepared for the extravagant material demands of industrialized warfare. As the armies of Europe settled into the stalemate of late 1914, military officers saw their accustomed tactics of movement and maneuver removed from their place in the natural order. Only mass and firepower remained. While it is too simplistic to say that the war became entirely a contest of industry, clearly massive production, whether in ships, shells, troops or saw blades, provided the mass and firepower that became, for the generals of Europe, the opening argument of victory. The profligate expenditure of artillery, millions of shells during single battles in 1916, strained the industrial capacity of virtually the entire world, threatening to bankrupt nations and permanently change the social order. Among those governments that survived, principles, paradigms and planning all lay prostrate before the imperatives of production.

This study will demonstrate that the reactions of both the Russian government and organs of Russian society to the challenges of the First

World War provide compelling evidence that neither group could effectively guide Russia through the challenges of the new century. In their efforts to secure supplies in the United States, both groups faced similar and approximately equal challenges. The government bureaucracy proved unable to address the crisis of wartime industrial production. The emerging liberal "civil society," laboring under far fewer restrictions in the United States than in Russia, still proved no more capable than their bureaucratic counterparts in dealing with industrial production and American capitalists. For all sectors of society, the war provided a hothouse of intensive activity and experience and a rich opportunity to evaluate their efforts.

The Government

Industrial warfare demanded an efficient means of administration. The Russian bureaucracy, immortalized in the characters they contributed to Russian literature, comprised a bewildering range of ministries, organs and councils. Their authority and loyalties often shifted based on personalities and prestige. Yet, in addressing the effects of the Tsarist bureaucracy on purchasing in America, the imperatives that transcended organizations permit the bureaucracy to be grouped as a common element.

All parts of the Russian bureaucracy traced their lineage to Peter the Great and the absolutist state that he created, in which the concept of rights was meaningless. Whether serf or noble, all persons were equally subjects of the Tsar; even noble status was always subject to the authority of the sovereign.[4] To the end of the empire, privileges, whether land, titles, or serfs, were ostensibly granted in return for state service. Privileges recognized past service and provided the resources for continued efforts, and could be removed when their use no longer pleased the sovereign. Until such judgment, the Russian noble answered to no one outside his own "chain of command" for his privilege and position. The Russian bureaucracy was born with a similar inherent territorialism. An office and its attendant responsibility became not only honorable employment, but also a valued possession as a means of social advancement; and office holders vigorously defended their authority. The resultant bureaucrat ruled his ministry with the autonomy of a noble on his country estate.

Despite this independence, the vast majority of state servants were poorly paid, overworked and little honored. The Russian bureaucracy was surprisingly small for its impression on the public mind. Throughout the nineteenth century, Russia had approximately twelve civil servants per 10,000 subjects, while much of Europe during the same period averaged three to four times more *per capita*.[5] The endemic bribery and corruption so often attacked by western observers was, in fact, an accepted part of the system of administration. Despite various attempts to establish acceptable salaries for civil servants, the Russian civil service never received more than a living wage, and often much less. The pay tables established in 1865, for example, remained unchanged for over thirty years. Such pay handicapped the recruitment of talented people, particularly professionals and university graduates. At the beginning of the First World War, only 51 percent of the senior Ministry of the Interior bureaucracy had attended a university. The resultant bureaucracy was poorly equipped to administer a growing industrial society, and was at the same time supporting itself by the Muscovite tradition of feeding itself off official business.[6] With corruption both an accepted facet of the job and, in some cases, a requirement for living, it can hardly be surprising that Russian wartime contracts, both at home and abroad, were characterized by what their Allies considered graft of the basest sort.

The final handicap facing the Russian bureaucracy was the idea that all subjects of the Tsar were equal in their subordination. In a state of such equality, there could be no central directing voice other than that of the tsar. Rather, each minister enjoyed the jealously defended right to address the tsar personally, insuring that only the sovereign could be in a position to direct and coordinate the efforts of the various ministries.[7] Relations between the key ministries of war, foreign affairs and finance were colored by a constant jockeying for the tsar's attention, and lines of organizational authority were often unclear. One scholar, for example, has commented that before the war, "the Russian Foreign Ministry was a major actor in the foreign policy-making process ... [but] it was never the dominant one."[8] Decisions were typically made at the most senior levels within each ministry, and the average career bureaucrat was granted little latitude in executing policy.

Civil Society

During the last ten years, the extent and efficacy of civil society in late Tsarist Russia has emerged as one of the most compelling questions of Russian historiography. With the demise of Soviet power, those who would create democratic institutions in modern Russia have struggled to place their efforts in historical context. If the late Tsarist period saw a growth in effective civil institutions, then the institutions established after the "interruption" of Communism can be seen as the continuation of a native process, rather than an unprecedented and foreign construct. The result has been the rebirth of the arguments of the post-revolution Russian liberals in more sophisticated form.[9]

The eclectic mechanisms through which independent "civil society" typically arose and sought expression—the press and literature; common associations of professions, concerns and pastimes; and ultimately political action—were all controlled and even proscribed in Imperial Russia.[10] The ostensible unity of the nation and the Tsar rendered the idea of associations of citizens independent of the sovereign a philosophical impossibility for the government. Further, as Walkin observed, "In an autocratic state trying to hold down a seething populace, there is no such thing as a harmless form of association."[11]

Despite this fact, elements of civil society did exist in Tsarist Russia. The last decades of the Russian Empire saw the emergence of a number of voluntary organizations of a political, social and professional nature which challenged government primacy in their areas of concern. While the intellectual underpinnings of civil society were not the result of government policy, these urges found expression in part through mechanisms created by the state during the "Great Reforms," the period of intense government reform which followed the Russian defeat in the Crimean War.

The most significant large scale expression of civil society was the zemstvo movement. Born out of the Zemstvo Act of 1864, the zemstvos, with their urban counterparts, established in each area of the empire a local assembly and a smaller executive board, both selected by election and entrusted with limited authority over local affairs. Voter eligibility was established by property qualification. As originally conceived, the zemstvos seemed to offer the hope of local self-government and were an outlet for a number of improvement initiatives. The nobles who were drawn to the new boards were largely activist in attitude and immediately began exceeding the limited government vision for the new institution.[12] As the zemstvos continued, the elected boards often secured the services of the emerging Russian professional classes to carry out their mandate. This "third element" of medical and legal specialists, educators, social scientists and statisticians was often more liberal and vocal than its more established employers.

The reigns of Alexander III (1881–1892) and Nicholas II (1892–1917) saw a government in retreat from the full implications of the Great Reforms. In 1889, the government instituted a system of land captains in an effort to reassert direct state control over peasant affairs. These state-appointed bureaucrats assumed many duties previously carried out by the zemstvos. As Nicholas II took the throne he reiterated his father's policies, cautioning those "people, who have been carried away by senseless dreams of the participation of zemstvo representatives in the affairs of internal administration" to expect no sympathy from the crown.[13]

Despite this legacy of government suspicion, Russian civil society had achieved a measure of recognition within specialized areas. By 1914, the liberal leaders of Russian society could point to real, if limited, successes in the political and economic realm as a result of their efforts.[14] For the organs of civil society, primarily the Unions of Zemstvos and Towns, the exigencies of the war represented freedom from the restrictions which had dogged their work. From its first efforts, the zemstvo movement had found its charters, granted in moments of state liberalism, strictly interpreted to limit its efforts to as narrow a field of action as possible. The legitimacy of the movement centered on the perception of zemstvo competency, even in the narrow field of support to the rural countryside. Where the government could not offer effective public health solutions, the zemstvos could train and equip *feldshers*, paramedical field practitioners, to care for the rural citizen. Where the government could offer only a vague estimation of the rural population, statisticians employed by the zemstvos produced detailed information on the Russian land. The Russo-Japanese War saw zemstvo activity expand into care for military wounded. With the opening of the First World War, military medical care would provide the entrée to a seemingly unlimited range of opportunities. By serving the war effort as patriotic Russians, civil society sought to underscore the efficacy and thus the legitimacy of its organizations.

Industry

Within the context of this study, Russian industry plays two distinct roles. First, the inability of Russian industry to produce sufficient munitions during the First World War created the need for overseas orders. While the Russian case was extreme, both Britain and France experienced similar failures. In general, these failures were the result of the widespread misunderstanding of the demands of industrial warfare and were not particular to Russian experience.

Second, the organized representatives of Russian industry functioned as a distinct element of Russian civil society. Organized representation of Russian industry was a more recent development than the zemstvo movement. In general, the long history of mutual interaction rendered industrial organizations less suspect in the eye of the government than social organs such as the zemstvos. Count Serge Witte, the influential minister of finance, had encouraged the development of representative organizations of industrialists and had used these organs to provide input to official policy.[15]

The State Duma and other government institutions that emerged in 1906 presented a new venue for political action. Despite state efforts to encourage industrial development, Russian industrialists typically believed that the state was biased against industry, if only from a lack of understanding. The concern in industrial circles was that the new Duma would be dominated by agricultural interests, and that only organized action could insure a sympathetic hearing of industrial needs. While some elements of the industrial community attempted to form a political party, their efforts ultimately coalesced into a nationwide Association of Industry and Trade.[16] This association would be active in Russian supply efforts in America during the First World War.

About the Text

By means of introduction, Chapter 1 of this study begins by outlining the disorder that characterized the first Russian supply efforts in the United States during 1914. Through this early period of the war, the full demand for military supplies had not yet been felt. Each Russian ministry conducted its own overseas purchasing, with only the barest pretenses of coordination. Chapter 2 describes how these efforts were transformed by the shell crisis of 1915. The Russian government, like its British and French counterparts, failed to anticipate the artillery requirements of the renewed military operations that followed the first winter of the war. The haphazard placement of the previous year's orders insured that this gap in supply could not be filled in the short term from overseas, despite the considerable funds that the Russian government had invested in these contracts. It was in the face of this government failure that representatives of the zemstvos and industry were incorporated into the formal overseas purchasing process.

The Russian government's institutional inability to control and organize its own overseas orders caused the British government to embark on a series of increasingly coercive measures to impose order on the process. The capacity of American industry to produce specialized products such as shells, cartridges and railroad engines was large but finite, and the British were acutely aware how the competitive purchasing practices of the Russian government disrupted the market and increased costs. As described in Chapter 3, Russian dependence on British funding provided both the carrot and stick for what ultimately proved ineffective reforms. Russian purchasing reached its most mature form, described in Chapter 4, during mid-1916. Even with formal control mechanisms in place, Russian representatives conducted their affairs with an independence that thwarted organizational efforts. Chapter 5 departs from the chronological progression to examine in detail a single order placed by zemstvo representatives in United States with the American Locomotive Company. Apologists for Russian liberalism have proposed that the failure of Russian wartime supply was caused strictly by government failures. The American Locomotive Company order was controlled entirely by zemstvo representatives in the United States, yet it experienced delays and mismanagement comparable to any government-administered contract. Chapter 6 discusses the ascendance of the Russian liberal elements after the February Revolution and the American entry into the war, while Chapter 7 concludes as the Supply Commission struggles to deal with the collapse of the Provisional Government.

The Library of Congress transliteration system has been used throughout this work with the exception of names of those Russian representatives who adopted as their own a specific transliteration during their work in the United States and Britain. Dates are given in the Gregorian (new) style throughout, with the few exceptions in the Julian (old) style indicated in the text. During the twentieth century, the Julian calendar ran thirteen days behind the Gregorian calendar. Doing business with the Allies, most Russian representatives abroad used the Gregorian calendar in their papers.

"The truth, however, will always remain that this new prolongation of the fighting in the east is mainly due to the furnishing of guns and ammunition by America..."

—Berlin *Tageblatt*, 1916

"The Russians are certainly a strange people."

—Edward R. Stettinius, 1917

"My generation was in the sweep of the avalanche."

—Boris A. Bakhmeteff, 1927

1

The Early War Orders

During the first months of the war, Russian government agents secured contracts for military supplies in almost every non-enemy industrial power on the globe. For all the energy these representatives expended, however, the lack of coordination between Russian agencies caused their efforts to be largely ineffective. As each ministry was competing for resources with no arbitrating authority, the largest share of funding went to the ministries that moved quickly to secure and spend available funding for their own needs. No effort was made to prioritize orders according to military need. Further, this competition encouraged the placement of orders quickly, often before contractors could be screened. As a result, early Russian orders were poorly planned and usually poorly executed.

The coming of war to Russia was greeted with an outpouring of support for the conflict, both spontaneous and official. Crowds filled the streets of St. Petersburg (soon to be renamed Petrograd), while a growing wave of labor unrest was abruptly, if temporarily, halted in the capital.[1] The State Duma met on July 26, 1914, in a one-day extravaganza of official support for the war. During the session, the Octobrist Duma chairman, Mikhail Rodzianko, asserted that "the war has put a sudden end to all our domestic strife [for] the Russian people has not known such a wave of patriotism since 1812." Similar expressions were made by representatives of the other major parties, with the five Bolshevik deputies providing the only open dissent. This truce between branches of government, which Kadet leader Paul Miliukov later dubbed the "*union sacrée*," represented a temporary change to the political landscape. "In no sense is the faction changing its attitude towards questions of internal affairs," he said, "only postponing the parliamentary struggle until the general and national danger has passed."[2] Overall, this stage-managed production presented to international audiences a picture of almost perfect unity.

In this unity, the national zemstvo movement perceived political opportunity. Acting in haste to preempt any government proscription, the movement gathered representatives of thirty-five local councils in Moscow on July 30, 1914. Between personal representatives and messages to the convention, every zemstvo in Russia except one elected to join an organization for the relief of the wounded. The organization was dubbed the "All-Russian Union of Zemstvos," and its president, Prince Lvov, again hastened to the Tsar to obtain his blessing. Approximately a week after the initial Moscow meeting, he explained to Nicholas that:

> A Central Committee has been formed at Moscow, and provincial and district committees locally. The whole organization has been built, not according to rigid and elaborate statutes, but on the basis of a powerful desire for collaboration. Out of their own resources, the zemstvos have been able to assign 12,000,000 rubles for the relief of the wounded. Our function is to receive the wounded from the army, transfer them to the hospitals, heal our wounded soldiers and then send them back to their homes.[3]

That Nicholas expressed his support for the effort was unsurprising. Whatever his subordinates' misgivings about the voluntary associations, the Tsar could hardly stifle such a patriotic effort. The zemstvo effort was echoed by the newly formed All-Russian Union of Towns in August, and shortly after the two unions agreed to consolidate their relief efforts. This united front came to be known as the "Zemgor," although the zemstvos remained the dominant members of the union throughout the war.

While civil society organized for the war effort, the Russian government implemented its existing military plans for continental war. Thirty-five reserve infantry divisions were mobilized to augment the seventy-nine active units. The distances involved and the lack of transportation left the Russian mobilization timetable substantially behind that of Germany and Austria-Hungary. Nonetheless, by the second month of the war, Russia planned on supporting a field force of 5,300,000 troops.[4]

Russia had made a concerted effort to stockpile munitions to support these forces. The Tsarist government actually entered the First World War with an excess of 3 inch artillery shells according to the 1910 reserve standard. Similarly, the War Ministry met the 1910 goals for the total number of artillery pieces on hand. Significant deficiencies still existed, however, in reserves of heavier artillery shells.[5] The immediate artillery deficiencies of World War I were not failures of the industrial base, but of military planning.[6]

As during the previous national emergencies, the Russian government expected to rely on foreign suppliers to augment domestic limitations. This wartime shift to foreign suppliers ran counter to the ostensible Russian policy of employing domestic manufacturers. This policy had been codified by Imperial decree as early as 1860, and had been reaffirmed in 1866, 1885 and 1900, but beyond expressing official policy it put no formal constraints on individual ministries placing foreign orders until 1902. Witte established a special commission to enforce the "Buy Russian" policy. The resulting regulations stipulated that overseas orders could only be placed for goods not produced in Russia. Orders for which Russian manufacturers could not meet official specifications or which they declined could also be placed abroad. In accepting a state contract, a Russian manufacturer was required to use Russian materials if available.[7] While the military in general seems to have been little affected by the new regulations, the 1902 rules severely restricted the thriving trade in American railroad engines and rolling stock. The committee that granted exceptions for foreign purchases worked almost entirely in the interests of an organized cartel of suppliers and not only routinely declined to approve foreign orders, but prohibited performance guarantees in domestic contracts. As a result, Russian locomotives were on average 3,000 rubles more expensive than foreign engines, while freight cars were typically 300 rubles more expensive than an imported unit.[8]

The effort to modernize Russian small arms during the 1890s represents a good example of the Russian attitude toward overseas military contracts. In 1891, the Russian Army adopted a modern, fixed-magazine, bolt-action rifle, which fired a smokeless powder cartridge, to replace the 1868 model. These Moisin-Nagant rifles were produced at three state-owned arsenals using machine tools largely imported from foreign firms. To supplement the slow production start-up and expedite the distribution of the new rifle, the War Ministry contracted with the French manufacturer Châtellerault for over 500,000 Russian-pattern weapons. Their delivery was delayed by the failure of the ministry to provide the agreed-upon manufacturing dies, but by April 1895 the entire order was fulfilled. With the initial need met, all subsequent Moisin-Nagant rifle production before World War I was conducted at the three state arsenals.[9]

The failures of the Russo-Japanese War reinforced the use of foreign suppliers. During the first year of the war, the Russian field commander, General Aleksei Kuropatkin, requested a range of supplemental weapons and ammunition, including 25,600 melinite explosive filled shells and 18,000 6 inch howitzer shells. None of the shells and very few of the requested weapons were ever delivered.[10] To make up for these shortfalls, the Ministry of War placed 16.9 million rubles in orders abroad during the first year of the war, as opposed to 2.3 million rubles the previous year. In 1906, foreign orders in the War Ministry quadrupled to 73.1 million rubles.[11]

Russia, however, conducted its foreign purchasing on a ministry-by-ministry basis. The natural habit of the Russian bureaucracy was to defend this prerogative, and the money and control which accompanied it, despite any effort to centralize purchasing. Even within the War Ministry, the *Glavnoe Artilleriiskoe Upravlenie* (Chief Artillery Directorate) remained virtually an independent entity with regard to foreign purchasing. While the organization of Russian purchasing never moved beyond the rudimentary stages, the first months of the war were anarchic even by Russian standards.

The initial Allied purchasing effort focused on raw materials such as copper, wax, lead and wool and equipment such as shoes, horses and finished clothing. The demand for munitions would not be fully apparent until spring 1915, and the long time required to tool plants for munitions production insured that the bulk of American exports to Russia during 1914 was not finished arms.[12]

The Shcherbatskii Commission

One of the initial Russian supply efforts was headed by Acting State Counselor Shcherbatskii and was nominally attached to the Russian Embassy. The so-called Shcherbatskii Commission was an *ad hoc* creation, staffed largely by embassy personnel and, as a later commentator said, locally available Russians of the appropriate class. The implication was that purchasing military supplies would be a collateral duty, added to official or business employment. Ustinov, the Russian consul general in New York; Vice Consul Baron O. A. Korf; and K. P. Sherchenko, his aide, ran most of the operation. The latter two gentlemen very quickly became the center of the commission, as the remaining members either lived in other cities or were too senior to become involved in the details of contract negotiation. The commission had no authority to authorize orders, but instead forwarded information to the appropriate agency in Petrograd. Korf and Sherchenko were quickly overwhelmed.[13]

Within the first months of the war, a number of businessmen had determined that quick profits could be had by acting as a middleman for the Allies. J. P. Morgan would later refer disapprovingly to this "...vast horde of 'war brokers'" that at once facilitated and complicated early war purchasing efforts.[14] Ideally, the broker performed the valuable service of bringing together the disparate Allied purchasers with American businesses. Perhaps typical of these firms was Gaston, Williams and Wigmore. Drawn by the war's opportunities, Gaston and Williams had come to New York from Cleveland, while Wigmore had been a local stockbroker before the war. Gaston operated in London, while the remaining principals maintained offices on Broadway. Established in September, by the beginning of December the firm had placed $12 million in Allied orders.[15]

The complexity and scope of the Allied requirements, however, were beyond the experience of almost all American businessmen. Worse, the vast sums of money involved quickly attracted speculators and outright frauds. Some attempted to buy up supplies in anticipation that the ongoing war would drive up the price the Allies would be willing to pay. In November 1914, a Washington lawyer in New York to find a buyer for 40,000 horses encountered a number of brokers:

> who want to purchase anything in the nature of war supplies.... If they find out that I have horses, they want me to give them an option on them for two or three days. When I ask them to take me to the real man who has the contract, they admit that they cannot do that at once, but their relations with that person are of such a close and confidential nature that they can do anything, but it will take a little time.... When I ask to be put in touch, they say they will consult their clients and disappear. Later comes a telephone call, which gives the information that their man has gone to Washington. If I will give them absolute carte blanche in the matter, they will purchase the horses and equipment from me.[16]

The New York papers carried notices from various embassies and missions, occasionally on the front page, disowning various supposed official purchasing representatives.[17]

Like the other Allies, the Russians suffered from a number of unofficial representatives who confused and exploited the purchasing situation. One prominent example, Ivan Narodny, was a naturalized American citizen of Russian birth and a self-described "political refugee." In 1914, he represented himself as an agent of the Moscow firm V. V. Agafononv. He made considerable press for himself by publicly announcing that the Russian Admiralty intended to purchase two American-produced submarines—by implication, with himself acting as the broker. He also alleged that he had placed orders for 900 tons of rails and 700 tons of armor plate on behalf of the Russian government. The report was taken seriously enough that Secretary of State William J. Bryan commented that building submarines in the United States for a belligerent would be a breach of neutrality.[18] Narodny established himself as managing director of the Russian Chamber of Commerce, one of the many wartime organizations promoting Russian trade. The Russian consul in New York eventually issued a warning that Narodny had "absolutely no connection with any departments of the Imperial government." Narodny responded that this denunciation was a result of his radical politics and refusal to bar Jews from the Russian Chamber of Commerce.[19]

It was against this haphazard backdrop that the Russian government entered the market for icebreakers in North America. The transport of foreign goods to Russia was an immediate concern and would become a driving issue in Russian supply throughout the war. While the Royal Navy was able to secure England's supply lines to North America, the Mediterranean and India, the German High Seas Fleet effectively cut the major merchant route through the Baltic Sea to Petrograd. With the exception of occasional passages by Allied warships, the Baltic would remain closed throughout the war. The next closest port to North American suppliers was Arkhangel'sk, located in northern Russia inside the White Sea. In 1914, Arkhangel'sk was a small port used principally for import of British coal. More importantly, however, the Gorlo Strait froze each year from December through March, closing the port. The Russian government had never before required the port to sustain year-round operations and realized the need to secure icebreakers to avoid closure. As an issue affecting the importation of goods, the requirement fell to the Ministry of Commerce, where it received high-level attention.

The urgent requirement to purchase two large icebreakers was passed to the Russian embassy in the United States, where it fell to Constantine J. Medzikhovsky, the commercial attaché. From a bureaucratic standpoint, the commercial attaché, as the ministry's representative, was the logical choice. However, prior to the war, Medzikhovsky had been primarily occupied with the encouragement of trade between America and Russia; his files reflect questions on tariffs and the *bona fides* of corporations. After the war began, his work shifted to answering American questions on Russian export restrictions and securing the necessary certificates for American companies to purchase Russian raw materials. Certainly the purchase of two ships was new ground for him.

While Medzikhovsky would ultimately prove a true "jack-of-all-trades" for the Russian war effort, his role as ship broker posed more problems than simple unfamiliarity. As a diplomat accredited to the embassy, his direct involvement in a military supply issue raised the specter of violating international laws concerning neutrals. Perhaps the fact that the icebreakers, while for wartime government service, were not to receive naval commissions was thought to avoid these concerns. The American respect for the forms of neutrality, however, was strong, and there was significant domestic opposition to any American trade with combatant nations. Even as Medzikhovsky was striking his first deal, the British government was consciously keeping the nascent British purchasing mission completely separate from their diplomatic structure to avoid such issues.[20] The Russian government would ultimately follow.

The war was hardly a month old when Medzikhovsky found his first icebreaker in Canada. Responding to the prospect, the Russian minister of commerce telegraphed, instructing the attaché to "go immediately [to] Montreal for inspection with expert ... if satisfactory sign contract."[21] What Medzikhovsky had found was the S.S. *J. L. Horne*, owned by the Great Lakes Dredging Company for use on Lake Superior and available for transit to Arkhangel'sk in five weeks. After his inspection, he traveled to Ottawa, where he appealed to the Canadian government to loan a second icebreaker to the Russians. While no loan was forthcoming, the Canadians were willing to sell the Canadian Naval Service Icebreaker *Earl Grey* for £100,000.[22] The Russians accepted both vessels and within a month had transferred funds for the *Earl Grey*. With the transfer, Medzikhovsky asked the Canadian government to "use all means" to expedite the sailing of the *Earl Grey* as the Russians feared that without it navigation to Arkhangel'sk would be closed in the coming winter.[23]

With the vessels secured, the next logical step was to hire crews willing to sail them through the war zone. Unfortunately, too many authorities set out to answer the need. In early October, Furness, Withy and Company, the shipping line outfitting *Horne* for its journey, wrote Medzikhovsky to say that, to their surprise, a Russian master, Captain Wimbe, had arrived with a crew for the steamer. Wimbe, they wrote, "was making considerable difficulty about crossing on her ... he claims that the boat cannot make the voyage safely." Asking that the attaché travel to Montreal and sort the matter out, they commented that "we are satisfied that nothing ... will be done with him until you have seen him."[24] The company's confusion surrounding Wimbe and his crew was understandable. When the matter was clarified, it emerged that the newly established Russian Government Committee in London, at the behest of the Ministry of Commerce, had contracted through R. Martins and Company, an English firm handling most of that committee's shipping issues, to secure personnel for the vessel. Furness, Withy and Company, contracted by Medzikhovsky, had no warning before the crew arrived from England. It is not clear which crew was aboard when the two vessels finally departed Canada in mid-October. *Earl Grey*, probably with a Canadian Naval Service crew, arrived in Arkhangel'sk without difficulty, where the Ministry of Commerce renamed her the *Kanada*. The *Horne* made an unscheduled stop in Halifax, where Furness, Withy and Company sent a new master. The replacement dismissed Captain Wimbe and had him arrested, seemingly on charges that he had declined to sail his vessel to Arkhangel'sk. Wimbe telegraphed Medzikhovsky, pleading that he had "not declined or refused to proceed to Arkhangel'sk with the *Horne* [but] was forced to put in here [in Halifax] owing to crew refusing to proceed."[25] Presumably, *Horne* reached Arkhangel'sk under its new master.[26] Medzikhovsky would continue his icebreaker purchasing efforts into mid-1915, securing at least one more vessel, S.S. *Lintrose*, for service.[27]

The continuing orders for the port of Arkhangel'sk indicate the seeds of Russian failure. The Ministry of Commerce followed the Canadian icebreakers with a series of orders for barges in November, wharves in December, railway improvements in January, additional icebreakers in February, a floating dock in April and so on. Even here, where one ministry was charged with a task, it failed to produce a comprehensive plan to prioritize and carry out the expansion of the port. Instead, the ministry addressed each of these orders to the Council of Ministers as an extraordinary expenditure, thwarting any attempt at budgeting.[28]

Medzikhovsky's experience, however, also pointed out several broader perils of the early Russian war orders. Concerns over embassy personnel conducting war purchasing would be relieved by upcoming bureaucratic changes, but Russian contracts would continue to be plagued by difficulties between contractors and Russian technical personnel. While Captain Wimbe is the only Russian on record as being arrested, other manufacturers certainly would have coveted a similar opportunity to be relieved of their Russian technicians. The lack of coordination between the triangle of authorities and agents in Petrograd, London and America would continue, and high-priority orders would continue to suffer as a result.

This triangle of authority became a pivotal issue in the Russian orders placed with the Canadian Car and Foundry Company during the first year of the war. These orders, because of their size and the extent of difficulty they ultimately presented to both Russian and British supply authorities, have become perhaps the most notorious of the Russian orders.[29] The orders were set in motion by an August 1914 request from Lord Kitchener to Sam Hughes, the Canadian minister of militia, for assistance in placing British orders in the Canadian market. Hughes, a Conservative politician who was not adverse to rewarding associates, recommended a friend, J. Wesley Allison, to oversee the effort. Allison, who would eventually be referenced in a British Foreign Ministry report as "the most notorious black-leg in Canada," was, in Hughes' plan, to be part of a committee to handle British purchasing in Canada.[30] Kitchener's reply to this enthusiastic proposal was ambiguous, and Hughes took that ambiguity as license. Hughes gave Allison an honorary commission as a Canadian militia colonel and transmitted to the Russian ambassador in Washington that:

> The Minister of Militia and Defense for Canada ... has officially instructed Colonel J. Wesley Addison [*sic*] to aid the allies in every way possible in purchases of requirements at lowest prices wherever his services are required.[31]

Allison first sought to interest the Russian ambassador to the United States in his services. He was rebuffed, but the defuse nature of Russian purchasing authority left him alternatives. With his blank check from Hughes, Allison traveled to London, where he installed himself in the Savoy Hotel and negotiated orders for the "Canadian Purchasing Syndicate." His efforts were eventually brought to the attention of Sir Robert Borden, the Canadian prime minister. Because of Allison's connections to Hughes and Hughes' stature within the ruling Conservative party, Borden could pass only an informal warning against doing business with Allison to the acting Canadian high commissioner in London.

Meanwhile, an associate of Allison, Colonel Herbert Mackie, traveled to Petrograd and achieved enough success in official circles to allow Allison to represent himself in London as an agent of the Russian government. Such was the disorder in Russian governmental affairs that the actual Russian representatives in Britain had difficulty determining his true status. Despite their questionable *bona fides*, Allison and Mackie succeeded in securing a Russian contract for 2 million shells, deliverable in August 1915.[32]

The Russian government was concerned enough in early 1915 to inquire of the Canadian government as to the chances of the contract being satisfied. By the time the Russian government thought to inquire, the Canadian government had closed ranks behind the deal. The lucrative war orders placed in the United States in 1914 produced the feeling in Canadian circles that Canadian industry was receiving a disproportionately small part of the war trade. The government also knew that Allison had brokered the Russian shell order to the Canadian Car and Foundry Company, a firm with strong Conservative political connections and a desire for war orders. The company had sent its own representatives to Petrograd in late 1914, and eventually secured orders for an additional 3 million shells. Thus, by March 1915, a firm with no experience in munitions held orders for 5 million urgently needed shells worth $82 million.[33]

By itself, Canadian Car could not satisfy the contract and quickly sought subcontractors in the United States. By April, details of these transactions reached the American markets. Under the headline "WE GET $21,724,400 ORDER FROM RUSSIA," the *New York Times* reported that several dozen American firms, in locations as diverse as Swanton, Vermont, and Kings Mill, Ohio, had received a total of $21,724,400 of the contract. Three American firms, American Locomotive Company, Pressed Steel Car Company and U. S. Cartridge, were each in negotiations for a $10 million share of the contract. While trumpeting American success in securing the contracts, the *Times* noted the complexity of the arrangements. The Russian government was required to advance funds to Canadian Car to finance the expansion of their plants necessary to fulfill the contract. Cash advances were to be held in escrow by the Canadian government until expended, or were to be returned to Russia if the war ended before being used. Further, the contract stipulated that, in the event of litigation over the contract, the Russian terms and not the English translation would be accepted.[34]

The New York Stock Exchange, which had closed for the four months following the outbreak of war in Europe, responded to the influx of war orders. Shares of firms engaged in war production, dubbed "war brides" by traders, increased dramatically. During one week in late April 1915, shares equal to 80 percent of all outstanding Westinghouse common stock were traded and trading volume was regularly exceeding one million shares a day.[35]

The April trading in Westinghouse stock was the result of rumors about the company's negotiation for a major Russian rifle order that ultimately, along with the Canadian Car shell orders, would be the centerpiece of Russian purchasing in America. With an acute need for small arms, the Russians placed two major orders with Westinghouse. The first, signed on May 24, 1915, called for the manufacture of 1 million rifles at a cost of $26.75 each. The second, signed on August 17, 1915, was for an additional 800,000 rifles at the same cost. Unlike Winchester, who received an order for 200,000 rifles in August, Westinghouse was not a rifle manufacturer. Westinghouse created a separate subsidiary, New England Westinghouse, to handle the enormous contract, and the Russian government advanced Westinghouse almost $12 million in British credits to finance the company's set-up costs. The first rifles were to be delivered six months after the signing of each contract.[36]

To American observers, the business climate made some American businesses too anxious in negotiations with the Allies. One merchant commented that his competitors "seem to forget ... that if the goods are not purchased here they cannot be got anywhere else with reasonable certainty...." American businesses had "a golden opportunity to make money now for the first time in years" but were "losing a good part of what should be theirs because of their too evident anxiety to get the business."[37] As J. P. Morgan later phrased the problem:

> ...the excessively depressed industrial conditions of 1913 and 1914 made many [American manufacturers] so eager for business that some were disposed to undertake munitions contracts without a full realization of their inherent difficulties.[38]

The difficulties of this complex web of inexperienced contractors and financial dependence would play out through the remainder of the war, and would become a major issue for the British, Canadian and Russian governments.

Where some may have been too anxious for trade, others realized the Allies' acute needs and seemed determined to demand the highest prices the market could bear. Allied purchasers quickly learned to be circumspect as to what their needs and funding were, and employed brokers as fronts in their negotiations. One of the primary benefits to using a broker to place orders for consumer goods was that the supplying firm would not realize it was in fact supplying a foreign government. Despite these precautions, the British government had its identity disclosed in the midst of several textile contract negotiations, only to find that the price demanded increased.[39]

The increased demand, potential profit and unfamiliar goods involved caused many orders to be placed with manufacturers with no experience in the production of munitions. "So strongly is the war-order fever raging ... that it is a rare industry that is not likely to find itself besieged to take an order...." The *New York Times* illustrated the situation by asking, "Who, for instance, would have thought that the Allies would ever discover the Owensboro Wagon Company at Owensboro, Kentucky, or that, having discovered it, they would overlook the fact that the company is in the business of making wagons?" Yet reports in New York indicated that the company had been offered a contract to produce 2 million rifles.

One report in June 1915 indicated that $30 million in war orders had not yet been placed. Firms refusing the work cited anti-war "sentiment, lack of mechanical equipment, low prices offered and severe specifications." Brokers were offering a 5 percent commission to anyone who could find a firm to accept an order.[40]

The execution of these early war orders was conducted in an environment of rumor and half-truths, born both out of ignorance and guile. In October, the *New York Times* noted that the Russian government was "figuring in a lot of business deals that are more or less mythical." The Russians had allegedly secured 1 million pairs of wool socks, ready for delivery in the stock of a local firm. Reliable wool dealers reported that no firm, and scarcely the entire market, could have satisfied such an order on short notice.[41] But in the slightly surreal world of the war brokers, any order could be plausible.

The tangled web of authorities maintaining supply representatives in America was to get worse before it got better. Unsurprisingly, American manufacturers did not hesitate to use Allied confusion and competition to increase prices. During early 1915, Britain, France, Russia and Belgium were each bidding for the limited American explosives production capacity. In one case, the British War Office had hesitated to sign a particular contract given the price quoted, only to have the Belgians purchase the entire lot at an even higher price. All four nations negotiated with Dupont, though the British withdrew from the proceedings when they discovered that the company was playing them against the Russians. J. P. Morgan and Company commented that the American market in metals and machinery had been "violently deranged" by the weight of Russian orders.[42]

Beyond the Byzantine maze of Russian purchasing authority, the larger and more complex problem of inter-Allied coordination loomed. Particularly during the early days of the war, each ally was attempting to place contracts with a limited capacity for military production. If not addressed, the prospect loomed of the Allies bidding up the price of war supplies to their collective detriment. French authorities had anticipated the problem less than a month into the conflict, when the French ambassador to Britain proposed a joint Anglo-French committee to coordinate Allied orders. Within two weeks, the board had expanded into the *Commission Internationale de Ravitaillement*, which the British administered as part of their Board of Trade.[43] Initially made up of Britain, France and Belgium, the board eventually included Serbia, Portugal, Japan, Italy and Romania.[44] As the Russians sought to expand their purchasing in Britain, it was natural that they be included in membership, if only because they could disrupt Allied supply efforts if excluded. The president of the Board of Trade commented that:

> If the Russian Gov't would make its purchases by the same method as the-French Gov't in conjunction with our Admiralty & War Office, we shouldby that means avoid competing against each other to our mutual detriment. We could moreover give [the Russians] full detailed information and suggestions as in the case of the French purchases.[45]

The Russians accepted the invitation, and detailed the commercial attaché to Britain, along with the military and naval attaches, as representatives to the committee.

Even as the *Commission Internationale de Ravitaillement* was being formed, the British and Russians established a separate Anglo-Russian Committee of Supply. Russian Ambassador Benkendorf attended its first meeting on September 27, 1914.[46] In January 1915, the Anglo-Russian Committee of Supply, along with the Russian representatives to the *Commission Internationale de Ravitaillement,* was folded into the newly established Russian Government Committee under General Timchenko-Ruban. The Russian Government Committee was to be the senior oversight board for the coordination of Russian orders abroad, a writ it never entirely achieved.[47]

The Sapojnikov Mission

Beyond the London-based committee, the Russians were attempting to organize purchasing in the United States. Seeing that the Shcherbatskii Commission was overwhelmed attempting to handle orders from the various ministries in Petrograd, the Russian ambassador appointed the embassy's military attaché, Colonel Nikolai Golevskii, to handle military orders in the United States. As Medzikhovsky's military counterpart, he was a logical choice.[48] Golevskii was an experienced officer who had served with the Twelfth Hussar Regiment and been awarded the Order of St. Vladimir, fourth class, for his service in Manchuria during the Russo-Japanese War. He spoke excellent, accent-free English, having been assistant military attaché in London from 1907 to 1912, and had been in America since 1913. During June and July 1914, he had visited Vera Cruz and Mexico City to observe American operations.[49] But nothing in his experience prepared him for the magnitude of the Russian supply effort. By September, Golevskii was established at the Hotel Vanderbilt in New York and completely overrun by the number of Americans seeking military contracts.[50] Further, even though he was a colonel and a General Staff officer, Golevskii was handicapped by his relatively junior status and constant need to refer decisions to Petrograd. In October, he wrote to explain these difficulties and request that Russian supply efforts in the United States be vested with sufficient seniority to permit decisions to be made without constant referral to Petrograd. Golevskii, however, would remain an important player in Russian military purchasing in the United States until his dismissal in late 1916.

In response to Colonel Golevskii's difficulties, Major General A. V. Sapojnikov was appointed to head Russian supply efforts in the United States. While primarily acting on behalf of the Ministry of War, Korf and Sherchenko also fell under his authority. Sapojnikov was later attacked for his style of living while in the United States. Prior to his arrival, the entire Russian supply effort was run from the Russian consul's office in the Flatiron Building in New York City, with a total expenditure of $350 per month, $300 of which was for a secretary. While this effort was totally inadequate, it provided a rather stark contrast against the cost of the accommodations General Sapojnikov took at the Waldorf-Astoria Hotel.[51] Sapojnikov made it clear in his reports to his superiors that his accommodations, as well as the numerous social engagements which occupied his time were essential "to save face before American society." Certainly as the officer controlling millions of rubles in Russian orders, Sapojnikov was on the guest list of every industrialist of consequence in the region.[52] Shortly after his arrival, Sapojnikov was involved in a serious automobile accident while on a social outing. The car hit a telegraph pole and rolled over, killing one passenger and injuring the others. The general was only slightly injured. His detractors contended that his official reports on the incident to Petrograd not only falsely stated that the accident occurred while the staff was performing official duties, but that the general had recommended himself for a wound badge for his injury.[53]

Beyond personnel problems, the Russians faced the problem of financing their war purchases. In many circles, the Russian need for outside financial assistance came as a surprise. Russia entered the war with the largest gold reserve in Europe, valued at some 1.7 billion rubles, a declining national debt and a trade surplus of 146.1 million rubles. In money, as munitions, however, the demands of war exceeded all projections. By the end of 1914, the Russian trade deficit would reach 141.9 million rubles. [54] In September, the Russian ambassador to Britain had proposed that a Russian line of credit of some £15 million, secured by either Russian State Bank gold reserves or treasury bonds, be made available. The British Treasury agreed to extend £20 million in credit, secured by £12 million in Russian treasury bonds and £8 million in gold to be shipped to Britain. The credit, however, came with strings attached. The August suspension of the redemption of Russian currency in gold had left Russian firms abroad with no means of securing foreign exchange, and a number of private Russian pre-war debts were going unpaid. The loan could be used for these debts or for purchases in Britain. At this point of the war, however, Britain was not prepared to finance Russian purchasing in America.[55]

This first attempt at British financial support illustrates two recurring difficulties for Anglo-Russian cooperation. First, the British government habitually attached conditions to the use of funds loaned to Russia. These conditions created resentment among the Russians, who, with some justification, pointed out that they were offering collateral and paying interest on these funds. They should be free to use them as they saw fit.[56] By 1916, British control of Russian financial support would be used to force the Russian government to coordinate its supply activities in North America. Second, the British insistence on physically shipping gold from Russia to Britain would continue to be a point of contention. Britain saw one of its primary roles in the Allied coalition as the maintenance of a stable, convertible currency that would give the Allies a ready medium of exchange in international markets. Of course, this role also continued the pre- and post-war British goal of maintaining the pound sterling as the standard of international exchange, and with it, British financial dominance. The gold transfers, which the British saw as essential to mutual Allied interest in a strong pound, looked to the Russians like British penury.[57]

As British restrictions drove Russia into American financial markets, Russia confronted three ongoing problems in dealing with American businesses. First, any trade or financial dealings were complicated by the lack of a trade agreement between the two nations. An 1832 trade treaty had been in force until 1911, when it foundered on an issue of equal protection for Jews. The treaty had required that the trade representatives from each nation be afforded the same protections as native citizens. The Russian government interpreted this article as requiring only that visiting American Jews be treated as a Russian Jew would be. Thus, American Jews attempting to do business in Russia were required to secure special permissions from the Interior Ministry and found themselves restricted to specific geographic areas. In December 1911, the House had voted 300–1 to end the treaty and the Taft Administration had complied.[58] For Russo-American relations, the problem of Jewish rights would remain a stumbling block to trade relations throughout the war, particularly as the Russian government never understood the depth of American feeling over the issue. Ostracized in reaction to the treaty abrogation, the American ambassador resigned in 1912, and the post remained vacant until 1916.[59]

The second difficulty facing Russian trade efforts was the legal complication of American neutrality. The neutrality issue was particularly nettlesome in late 1914 as the American government had not yet defined its policies toward belligerents. Secretary of State William J. Bryan had argued that private American loans to any belligerent would oblige the United States government to permit loans to all belligerents, that such actions could divide the country between supporters of various hostile powers, and that the denial of credits to all sides would shorten the war. When J. P. Morgan and Company inquired as to the official view of loans to foreign belligerents, Bryan wrote that:

> There is no reason why loans should not be made to the governments of neutral nations, but in the judgment of this government, loans by American bankers to any foreign nation which is at war are inconsistent with the true spirit of neutrality.[60]

Robert Lansing, at the time a counselor for the State Department, argued that, since American citizens could enlist with belligerent armies, private capital should be no more restricted.[61]

The third issue was the strong isolationist tendency among American workers and businessmen. Even as brokers scrambled to placed lucrative war orders, a number of firms, particularly in the Midwest, refused to take munitions related orders. As Canadian Car was subcontracting their $83 million shell order, at least three Midwestern steel manufacturers declined the business, as "they did not care to participate in the manufacture of death-dealing implements of war."[62] While it does not seem that firms refusing munitions business ever approached a majority, their numbers were large enough to complicate the already tight steel and machinery market, and their refusals were often noted in the press.

While this internal disagreement played out, the Russian government was inquiring both formally and informally as to the availability of American capital. On October 20, 1914, Ambassador Iurii Petrovich Bakhmetev formally requested a statement of the U. S. government policy.[63] The request arrived as the State Department was considering a French request, made through the National City Bank of New York, for $10 million in credits for purchases in America. The bank and the French asserted that this proposal was different than previous rejected proposals, in that the funds were bank credits for purchases in America, in place of bonds being sold at large. The October 20 Russian proposal was also through National City Bank, and followed similar lines. In an October 23 meeting with Lansing, President Woodrow Wilson conceded the distinction between war loans and credits, offering that commercial credits were "merely a means of facilitating trade by a system ... which will avoid the clumsy and impractical method of cash payments."[64] This perhaps fragile distinction opened the door for what was to become millions of dollars in credits to the Russians.[65]

The host of American suppliers who were eagerly positioning themselves to fill Allied war needs strengthened the political case for credits. The Russian trade was regarded as particularly lucrative. The National Association of Manufacturers advocated making American credit available to Russia, convinced that failure would result in Russian war orders bypassing America for Britain.[66]

While the question of American financing was still being settled, however, the British Treasury had softened its stand on the British government loan to Russia. While primarily for British purchases, the Treasury agreed that funds could be spent outside Britain for items not available from British sources. The Russians, still balking at the gold transfer, accepted the £12 million loan backed by bonds, and the agreement was signed on October 26.[67] The loan was to prove less adequate than the Russians had hoped, and by December, the Russian government was seeking an additional £40 million loan from Britain, which was granted in January. During the first six months of the war, the Russian government received from Britain and the United States almost 1.39 billion rubles in credits for war supplies.[68]

The need for Allied financial coordination led to the first conference of Allied finance ministers, held in Paris on February 4–5, 1915. The Allies had realized that credit, like industrial capacity, was a finite resource, and that uncoordinated bidding for funds would create a similar rise in costs. In December 1914, a French banker doing business in Russia had proposed that combining all Allied credit requirements and guaranteeing them as a block would vastly simplify war finance. The Russians, with the weakest finances of the three major Allies, embraced the idea.[69] While the British and French embraced the principle, the question of implementation in light of Russian needs dominated the conference. The British conceded that depleting the Russian gold reserves would likely destabilize the Russian currency. Instead, the British proposed shipping Russian gold to London, where it would ostensibly remain part of the Russian gold reserve, but would be available as backing for Allied credits. Both Russia and France were each to provide Britain with £12 million in gold. The Russian government would be authorized to raise £100 million by issuing notes, backed by Britain and France, on the French and British financial markets. Until the offer could be made, the British and French governments agreed to extend Russia £25 million each, to be repaid from the proceeds of the offering.[70]

Beyond purely financial concerns, however, the British also broached the issue of coordinating orders placed in the United States. Even at this early date, the British were acutely aware of the competition between various Russian ministries. In response to a similar problem, Britain had commissioned J. P. Morgan and Company as their exclusive American representatives at the start of 1915 and proposed unifying all Allied purchasing in America through Morgan. Russian Finance Minister Peter L. Bark had already departed Paris when the question was raised, leaving Ignatiev, the Russian War Ministry representative, as the Russian spokesman. With no instructions on the matter, Ignatiev offered the view that Russia would insist on preserving its independence in purchasing decisions. As the French delegation was divided on the issue, Lord Kitchener proposed that the matter be postponed until the respective governments had approved the results of the main conference. In actuality, Bark had supported the idea of unified purchasing, but had not instructed Ignatiev on the topic. Ignatiev's instinct to defend bureaucratic prerogatives, however, was closer to the views of the Russian government, and Morgan never became an official Russian government representative.[71]

J.P. Morgan and Company

The role of J. P. Morgan and Company in British and, subsequently, Russian supply purchases in America forms one of the most unique chapters of the war. By trade, Morgan was a New York-based finance house, with associated firms in London and Paris. Though its key role in Allied finances was established virtually at the war's beginning, the firm had no experience in purchasing or manufacturing. Yet, as early as September 1914, the firm received a request from the French government to act as its agent in the purchase of ten thousand horses in the United States. Several months later, Henry Davison, the firm's London representative, received an unsolicited proposal from Lloyd George, then Chancellor of the Exchequer, that Morgan act as the sole British purchasing agent in North America. At the point of the proposal, the problems of British purchasing arrangements in North America had become evident. Britain was dealing with unfamiliar firms and had continual difficulties coordinating its contracting and financial efforts. Combining these functions in one firm of unimpeachable soundness and evident pro–Allied sentiments, intimately familiar with American corporations, would be a great boon to the supply effort.[72]

For Morgan, the unexpected offer required that the firm acquire a completely new set of skills. Morgan hired Edward R. Stettinius, an executive of the Diamond Match Company, to oversee the newly formed Export Department. As he later observed: "When the official announcement came on January 15, 1915, [that] the Morgan & Company had been appointed commercial agents for the British government, nobody realized what the duties would mean."[73] Morgan had so little appreciation for the scope of the enterprise which they had entered that Stettinius' initial appointment was part-time and his pay was a small commission on the contracts placed.[74] Stettinius himself took only a three month leave of absence from Diamond Match.[75] Whatever their original thoughts, Morgan quickly learned the nature of the British supply business. Stettinius recalled that, within days of the announcement, the firm was:

> overrun, not with hundreds, but thousands of people anxious to sell all kinds of things. There were manufacturers, both responsible and irresponsible ... merchants, commission agents, horse dealers, inventors, and war brokers by the score. After listening to ... the typical war broker, you would have thought that four or five million rifles, one or two billion rounds of rifle cartridges ... could be picked up almost anywhere for immediate delivery. Everything was in a state of chaos.[76]

While Morgan was never formally a purchasing representative of the Russian government in America, the British insistence that British funded orders be placed solely through them intertwined the fates of the firm and the Russian Supply Commission. Between 1915 and 1917, Morgan would handle 44% of all Russian orders from America.[77] Further, the Russian government would, like the French, use Morgan as a broker in a range of financial transactions.

On January 23, 1915, the Russian government concluded a $25 million credit arrangement with a group of New York banks. The money was intended to finance Russian war purchases in the United States over the following three months, with J. P. Morgan and Company acting as financial representatives in the deal.[78] While the cause and effect are unproved, this loan arrangement probably made possible one of the crowning achievements of the early Russian supply efforts in America. On January 24, 1915, the Russians signed a contract with the Remington Arms Company for 1 million Russian model 1891 rifles. It would remain one of the single largest deals of the war.[79]

If the Russians were willing to take Allied money, they were proving less willing to take Allied advice. In January 1915, the French government sent a technical mission to Russia to assist with shell production. After their inspections, the mission made four suggestions to the Russians: simplify the type of fuses being produced, relax inspection rules, militarize labor in the coal mines to insure a constant supply and reorganize the rail system to insure raw materials were always available. Only the first suggestion was even partially adopted.[80]

The peculiar specifications of some Russian equipment added to the difficulty in placing their contracts and the ultimate expense of the purchase. For example, an early 1915 order for 400 locomotive engines specified copper fire boxes. American locomotive manufacturers typically used steel in these parts, and pointed out the added expense to the Russians, as the 400 engines would require the use of 3.2 million pounds of copper. According to the Americans, no operational requirement precluded the Russians from using the cheaper steel parts—merely that long experience had made the Russians familiar with copper. The *New York Times* business column wryly reported:

> Anyway, Russia will have 1,000 tons of copper which she would not otherwise have had. She may eventually do what the Germans were reported to have done to replenish ammunition shells; that is, strip the locomotives of their copper fire boxes and substitute iron boxes.[81]

The Russians also continued to suffer from inflexible guidance placed on their negotiations by officials in Petrograd. The Pullman Company declined an early 1915 Russian order for 50,000 rail cars worth about $25 million because the contract would be paid in Russian government notes, in place of cash, and the cars would be required to be built in a plant Pullman would establish in Russia. When Pullman objected, the Russian agent indicated unsurprisingly that he was "without discretion in the matter."[82]

Statistically, the scope of Russian orders during the early period was impressive. By the end of 1914, Russia had placed orders for over $100 million in vital war equipment in the United States.[83] The absence of any coordinating body within the Russian government, however, insured that these orders were placed without regard to their priority for the war effort. Instead, each ministry acted in competition, seizing as much of the available capacity for its own needs as possible. Further, the competition between ministries for resources encouraged them to place orders quickly, before other agencies could obligate available funds. This arrangement produced a climate that discouraged careful screening of contractors.

In 1916, Colonel Golevskii would be asked what American trait he most admired. Without hesitation, he replied that it was "the remarkable energy of the American people." Or, he said, by way of example, "If you were to inquire of an American candy manufacturer, we'll say, 'Can you build an aeroplane?' the candy manufacturer would reply instantly, 'I'll try.' And what is more, he might build it."[84] The problem, of course, was that he might not—and a number of the early war orders involved firms working in just such unfamiliar territory. For all the reassuring contracts and ledgers, there was a vast gulf between placing orders for supplies and delivering the goods to the front. In spring 1915, the full scope of the difference would strike the purchasing effort, the Russian Army and the entire nation.

2

The Crisis Breaks

Russian purchasing agents in the United States had secured an impressive list of contracts during 1914. Most of these orders anticipated delivery beginning in the spring and summer of 1915. Russian agents, however, had placed most orders with firms largely inexperienced in munitions production, resulting in cost overruns and delays. The realization that Russian orders had been invested in firms not able to deliver struck the Russian government just as the shortage of ammunition became most acute.

Of five major powers heavily engaged in the opening of World War I, not one anticipated the incredible rate of munitions consumption that the war would demand. The mass employment of quick firing artillery, in particular, drained even the most extravagant pre-war reserves, leaving each of the three major Allies to experience a "shell crisis" during the spring of 1915. While military circles in Britain had known of shortfalls in shell supplies since the previous fall, the shell crisis sprang fully formed into the public conscience with the May 14 issue of the *Times*. Writing of the failed British attack on Aubers Ridge, the *Times* military correspondent wrote that the British "had not sufficient high explosive to level the enemy's parapets to the ground.... The want of an unlimited supply of high explosive was a fatal bar to our success."[1] The resulting furor contributed to the replacement of the Asquith government by a coalition cabinet and the installation of Lloyd George as minister of munitions.[2]

In Russia, as in Britain, military and governmental figures were reluctant to concede that the regime was failing to provide adequate munitions to the front. In an environment of increasing denial and avoidance, Minister of War General V. A. Sukhomlinov was particularly noteworthy in his refusal to admit to the shortages that were becoming increasingly apparent. The French ambassador in Petrograd, Maurice Paléologue, recorded on December 8, 1914, that he was "getting reports from many quarters that the Russian Army is running short of gun ammunition and rifles." In search of official information, he met with Sukhomlinov, who, he wrote:

> gave me a very friendly reception. Between his heavy eyelids a winking smile made the little wrinkles on his brows contract. His whole personality breathes physical exhaustion and deceit. I questioned him very closely. He kept on answering "Don't worry; I've prepared for everything," and he produced for me the most comforting figures.[3]

Nine days later, Grand Duke Nicholas, commander-in chief of the Russian Army, informed Paléologue that the Russian Army would be discontinuing offensive operations because of a lack of artillery shells. Paléologue met with Sazonov, the minister of foreign affairs, the same day to complain that:

> General Sukhomlinov has assured me a dozen times ... that all precautions had been taken to secure that Russian artillery should always have an abundant supply of ammunition.... I have emphasized to him the enormous consumption which has become the normal scale of battles. He ... vowed that he was in a position to satisfy all requirements and meet all eventualities. He even gave me written proof.[4]

The next day, he received from General M. A. Beliaev, the chief of staff of the army, something approaching a comprehensive view of the situation. Beliaev confessed to shortages in both rifles and artillery shells. In desperation, the Russian Army was "about to purchase a million rifles in Japan and America." Based on projected Russian production, the artillery situation would be desperate until March, when, Beliaev stated, "the deliveries on orders we have placed abroad will begin to arrive."[5]

Even after the official admission, getting information on Russian needs and priorities was a major frustration for the Allies. By March, the Foreign Office cabled the British ambassador that:

> [the British] War Office is still in the dark as to extent of the [Russian supply] problem. The whole scheme of military operations is thereby compromised. Isolated appeals for assistance are of no use to us or to Russia. We must have a full, frank, reasoned and exact statement of total Russian requirements with particulars as to all orders placed abroad....
>
> If the shortage is really serious, the present ... inability of the Artillery Department either to estimate its extent or to take measures against it is gravely disquieting....[6]

This admission drove the previously discussed series of orders placed in America during early 1915. The crisis, however, was yet to come.

By spring, the munitions crisis in Russia had been officially, if inconsistently, acknowledged to the Allies for some six month, but was still carefully concealed from Russian society. The general perception throughout the government and business communities was that the nation was best served by attempting to maintain pre-war production methods as far as possible, and that the natural functioning of business would provide for the country's needs. As Seman Zagorsky commented in 1928, "the aim of an economic policy was to leave everything unchanged, as it was before the War." Prior to the public outcry over the shell crisis, the government confined itself to expanding the army's right to requisition goods under an existing 1869 law. Not until September 1914 did the government require that factories fill military orders on a priority basis, where before businesses had the right to reject government work in favor of more profitable civilian orders.[7]

The Russian retreat from Galicia in May, followed by the virtual abandonment of Poland through the summer, however, forced the truth into public circles. The British military attaché, General Knox, recounted the experiences of a Guards battery commander:

> In the retreat infantry officers used to come to him to implore him to fire "just one or two shots" to help them ... and he had to refuse ... they sometimes asked, "Is it true what they tell us, that you have no shell left?" and he had to lie and say that it was not true, but that he was keeping the ammunition for a critical moment. Then they used to say, "All right, but when will that critical moment be if not now?"[8]

But even as the Russian Army was losing vast territories, Knox observed that "most Russian officers ... thought it was their duty to give me an optimistic view of the situation.... It was only months later that artillery officers told me of ... their powerlessness to help the infantry."[9] In fact, during the May breakthrough, the German Eleventh Army possessed a million shells, while the Russian Army opposing them held just over 100,000.[10]

The Government and the Crisis

In mid–May, several prominent Duma officials, including Chairman Rodzianko and the Progressist Deputy Efremov, returned to the Duma from the Galician Front. Their first-hand reports of the armament situation destroyed once and for all the myth that the regime was coping with the demands of the war.[11] Thrust into the public debate, the government, Duma and industrialists would all attempt to respond to the "shell crisis."

The official government response was weak and ineffective. During May 1915 Tsar Nicholas II made a personal visit to the front. Immediately prior to the Tsar's arrival, Duma Chairman Rodzianko had pressed Grand Duke Nicholas to support increased government control of armaments production. Upon hearing the Grand Duke's report, the Tsar summoned Rodzianko to headquarters. There, Rodzianko wrote, "the Emperor was pleased with the idea of a Special Council, and its outlines were drafted on the spot."[12] The Imperial *ukase* of May 19, 1915, formed a committee chaired by the minister of war and included Duma representation. The Duma, particularly the Kadet leadership, considered this an insufficient response and on June 7 the first committee was replaced in favor of a second, succinctly dubbed the "Special Council for the coordination of measures directed to the regular supply to the army of munitions and other materials during the present War." This special council was also chaired by the minister of war, and included the Duma president, four Duma deputies selected by the tsar and four representatives of the industrial community. While the special council was granted powers to requisition property and direct factory orders, these were essentially the same powers granted the minister of war in the fall of 1914. Other than the sop of Duma representation, the government had made no effective changes to its industrial policy.[13]

Civil Society and the Crisis

The most significant public impact of the shell crisis started in Russian industrial circles. The Ninth All-Russian Congress of the Association of Industry and Trade was held in Moscow in June 1915, even as Russian forces were yielding Galicia. The association seemed an unlikely venue for a radical solution to Russian supply problems. Officially committed to business as usual, the schedule for the Congress was little different from those of pre-war meetings. On the second day, however, Riabushinskii, the prominent Moscow industrialist, broke from the established agenda to recount his recent travels to the front. Based on the shortages he had seen among the troops, he issued a call for industrial commitment to the war. The scheduled discussions ended and the Congress addressed the "self-mobilization" of Russian industry.[14]

During the All-Russian Congress, industry labored to portray their "self-mobilization" as the correct and sufficient response to the crisis at hand. Resolutions called for the return of skilled laborers from the army, the unlimited use of Chinese workers in European Russia and the use of refugees in war production.[15] Most tangibly, the Congress established the Central War-Industries Committee. The committee consisted of nineteen departments, primarily separated by industry. Each department was further divided into sections specializing in some aspect of production. While the Central War-Industries Committee was approved at the Congress, what real effectiveness it had lay in the district committees that the Congress called on local industrial organizations to form. Over the next several months, the industrial movement formed some seventy-one local committees and twenty-eight provincial committees. These committees met in July 1915 to adopt a constitution and finalize the Central War-Industries Committee composition.[16]

The most prominent interpretation of the motivations behind the War-Industries Committees emphasizes the industrialists' economic motivations. The committees were largely made up of Muscovite industrialists who had been largely excluded from the large war orders that the Russian government had concentrated in the Petrograd area industrial concerns. Elements within the organization also believe the "self-mobilization" of industry would pre-empt any government move to nationalize production. At some point in 1915, the War-Industries Committees, however, elected to send representatives abroad, involving the committees directly in activity which was not of direct financial gain to the small firms and Muscovite industries they represented. In the United States, the Central War-Industries Committee appointed Professor Boris A. Bakhmeteff and S. I. Gavrilov, both engineers, as representatives, while P. A. Morozov served as representative for the Moscow War-Industries Committee. Ordered to the United States in August, they would become charter members of the Russian Supply Commission in America.[17]

The news from the front also had a profound effect on political developments in Russia. As in Britain, the first news of ammunition shortages at the front was followed by reports, some accurate and some sensationalized, that the crisis had been coming for some months. In Russia, stories took the ominous turn of questioning the loyalty of responsible officials, particularly War Minister General Sukhomlinov.[18] When the State Duma convened in July 1915, the major purpose of the sitting had become, in Miliukov's words, "to identify those responsible for this national disaster ... [to] condemn the mistakes, and maybe crimes, which have lost us not only Galicia, which cost us many lives, but ... maybe Poland."[19] For the moment, the "*union sacrée*" held, but it was clear that further government failures would increase the rift between liberal and governmental elements.

The Special Relationship Begins

In March 1915, the British offered the Russians a contract for 5 million shells with the American-based Bethlehem Steel Company, followed in April by a contract for 5 million shells which they had brokered with the American Locomotive Company. Despite their acknowledged need for shells, the *Glavnoe Artilleriiskoe Upravlenie* rebuffed both offers. Even when Lord Kitchener repeated the latter offer, the department expressed an intent to place no further foreign orders. According to the British military attaché, the department was "bitter" over orders placed with the British firm Vickers.[20] These orders for 1.2 million shells had been issued in November 1914, along with a 41 million ruble advance, for delivery in early 1915.[21] By April, the Russians had received no shells, and, as the spring campaigns pointed out their acute needs, understandably concluded that "there was nothing to be hoped for from other foreign firms."[22]

Kitchener was incensed at Russian accusations that Britain was not supporting its military efforts. In response, he provided the foreign minister with a memorandum outlining the ongoing British efforts. In one section Kitchener made clear his view that the lack of Russian supplies was entirely due to "the ineptitude of the Russian officials in not obtaining proper supplies of munitions."[23]

Determined that Russia needed foreign orders to sustain its war effort, Lord Kitchener bypassed the British military attaché and dispatched Colonel Wilfred Ellershaw to the *Stavka* (Russian Supreme Military Headquarters) with a personal letter for Grand Duke Nicholas. Ellershaw's visit in mid–May succeeded beyond all expectations when the grand duke, by this time immersed in the retreat from Galicia, appointed Lord Kitchener as "his agent for the purchase of shells, rifles and ammunition."[24]

Kitchener's ability to circumvent the considered decision of the *Glavnoe Artilleriiskoe Upravlenie* reflected the unique military structure of Russia during the war. Russia essentially possessed two separate and often contentious administrations; the civil administration, including the Council of Ministers and the War Ministry, and the *Stavka* and its subordinate forces. The line between the two groups was primarily geographic. Within the zones of military administration, the *Stavka's* authority extended, or could be interpreted to extend, to virtually all civil matters. Jealous of their own authority, and with a history of rivalry even before the war, the two groups quickly developed the habit of making major decisions without consulting the other.[25] While Sukhomlinov was a prime cause of the rift, his replacement in June 1915 revealed that the problem was institutional. The new war minister, General A. A. Polivanov, was soon complaining that "the *Stavka* ... [does] not communicate to the head of the war department any facts on the situation on the fighting lines."[26] For its part, the War Ministry had gained a reputation with the *Stavka* for ignoring its pleas for increased ammunition supplies. The situation was exacerbated by the Russian Army's logistical arrangements. Because each major military command under the *Stavka* was essentially a peacetime military district transformed into a field command, army logistics planning and organization thought in terms of the movement of supplies from the rear of the zone to the front. No established linkage existed between the logistics organization of the geographic area and the national economy; and the War Ministry, logically if not formally responsible, never created a satisfactory arrangement.[27] Given the situation, it is not surprising that the grand duke would elect to trust a British field marshal over his own War Ministry to secure munitions for his troops.

Receiving notice of this sweeping development, the Foreign Office issued a statement to the Russian foreign minister via the British ambassador that, while Lord Kitchener would attempt to secure munitions for Russia, His Majesty's government could give no guarantees, especially in light of the Russian refusal of the March and April contract offers. In response, the Russian Foreign Minister testily listed the millions of shells and fuses already ordered in Britain and Canada over the comment that "so far there has been no delivery."[28] The implication was clear. Russia needed Britain to expedite the contracts already let, not merely offer the opportunity to send more money abroad.

The *Commission Internationale de Ravitaillement* was certainly not the answer to the procurement problem. In February 1915, one of the British representatives commented that there was "no cohesion between the various Russian delegates, they all seem to take pride in each one going his own way and keeping his actions as secret from his colleagues as he possibly can."[29] While their own representatives were perhaps internally more cohesive, the other Allies also failed to employ the commission as intended. The original Anglo-French agreement establishing the organization had allowed each nation to continue purchasing through separate channels. The French Ministry of Munitions never used the commission, while the British Ministry of Munitions, once established, often ignored the organization because its British representatives were attached to the Board of Trade. As the Russians attempted to impose order on their own efforts, the Allies provided little inspiration. Unable to control new orders, the commission had no influence over the existing contracts.[30]

In May 1915, the Russians sent new leadership to Britain to attempt to expedite purchasing. Major General E. K. Hermonius and Colonel N. Beliaev both arrived in London as representatives of the *Glavnoe Artilleriiskoe Upravlenie*, but quickly expanded their influence beyond artillery orders. Hermonius, the one Russian praised by both his Allied contemporaries and the British official history, carried authority to resolve technical questions, primarily from Russian Supply Commission inspectors, which previously had been forwarded to Petrograd for decision. The measure of success he achieved in supply matters is more impressive considering that General Hermonius spoke no English.[31] His aide, in contrast, spoke English fluently, and had the additional benefit of being the nephew of General M. A. Beliaev, who was by this time serving as an assistant minister of war.[32]

Grand Duke Nicholas had requested that Kitchener find a way that Hermonius and Beliaev could control Russian purchasing in America.[33] Though Colonel Ellershaw's return from Russia and Hermonius and Beliaev's arrival occurred just weeks after the formation of the Ministry of Munitions, Kitchener's personal interest in Russian supply motivated him to maintain Russian supply as a separate issue within his own organization. The result was the War Office Committee for the Purchase of Russian Supplies. The panel originally consisted of seven members: U. Wintor, the British Director of Army Contracts; Colonel Ellershaw; a representative each from the Ministry of Munitions and the *Commission Internationale de Ravitaillement;* and General Hermonius, Colonel Beliaev and de Routkowsky as the Russian representatives. The official history of the Ministry of Munitions notes that the committee initially sought to place the Russian orders in Britain, but was forced to turn to the American market by a lack of industrial capacity.[34]

For the Russians purchasing supplies in the United States, the new arrangement kindled hopes of a veritable flood of British money, and initially the Russians were not disappointed. On May 17, 1915, the British, probably referring to the Kitchener's "appointment," informed Morgan that Russia had granted them "practically a free hand" to arrange munitions orders and that inquiries were to be made immediately. On May 21, the War Office expanded its guidance, noting that any reasonable additional cost necessary to insure delivery of shells before the end of the year would be approved. Orders for Russia were, Morgan was told, "the most urgent and vital of all the enquiries made through them."[35] By October 22, 1915, Morgan had placed £72 million in orders for Russia, with another £21 million authorized but not yet placed. This £93 million approached the £107 million in orders that Morgan had placed for Britain during the same period.[36]

The initial placement of these orders was fraught with difficulty. While later the question of inspection would become the major problem in Russian orders, there were early difficulties in securing the necessary Russian technical specifications required to conclude the contracts. In the words of the official history, "sometimes they had to be sent for from London, sometimes from Russia, and when, after delay prejudicial to negotiations, they finally arrived they were found to be in Russian." Morgan, usually the great expediter, refused to take responsibility for translation, and a number of orders waited for the arrival of a Russian government translation. While not entirely clear, the official history's reference to the "arrival" of the official translation suggests that the Russian Supply Committee in America did not, in the interests of speeding the war effort, undertake the translation itself. Whether it did or not, the official process was so extended that Morgan risked no little embarrassment by attempting to borrow the translated specifications from companies that already had Russian munitions contracts.[37]

The flood of British-funded Russian orders placed in spring 1915 was entirely placed in the name of His Majesty's government on behalf of the Russians. It was a unique legal arrangement and later caused difficulties in resolving conflicts over orders. After the war, the British portrayed the move as a necessary extension of the British purchasing arrangement with Morgan. The British insisted that Morgan negotiate all British-funded orders. Morgan, however, would not sign a contract for the Russians as the Russian government had never formally appointed them as their agents. Further, Morgan expressed doubts that American firms would honor the unsecured credit of the Russian government.[38] While these factors were true and argued for the British arrangement, the status of the contracts also served as a further guarantee of British control of Russian purchasing.

With the sum of British purchasing funneling through Morgan, not only did Russian and British interests conflict, but occasionally Russian interests worked against each other. In February 1915, J. P. Morgan and Company was forced to approach the Russian representatives in America and ask them to cease their inquiries after certain munitions. The British government had previously tasked Morgan to place orders for the same munitions for Russia.[39]

The difficulties continued. In March 1915, the British government complained that Russian representatives had been making inquiries for the purchase of toluol, a critical chemical ingredient in explosives, at prices above what the British were paying, and had made so many inquiries after small arms ammunition that firms were reluctant to quote British orders in hope of more lucrative Russian bids. Morgan reported that this state of affairs continued through at least June 1915, when Russian inquiries after shells had driven up the cost of zinc.[40]

The root of the problem was that General Sapojnikov, and with him, the balance of the Russian representatives in America, felt no obligation to observe the strictures of the *Commission Internationale de Ravitaillement* or standing Anglo-Russian arrangements with regard to their own purchasing. In an attempt to solve the problem, in July 1915, General Hermonius, accompanied by Colonel Ellershaw, made an inspection tour of Russian purchasing in the United States. In a parallel effort, the British Ministry of Munitions sent D. A. Thomas to the United States. The result was a temporary improvement in Russian purchasing arrangements in the United States, but, ironically, a financial problem for the British Exchequer. While in America, Hermonius, Ellershaw and Thomas brokered a contract with the Winchester Repeating Arms Company for 200,000 rifles. The contract was necessary, but the visitors had, like the permanent delegation so many times before, not considered the status of Russian credit before signing.[41]

One result of the Hermonius-Ellershaw visit was the appointment of a British Ministry of Shipping official to the Russian Transportation Committee. T. S. Catto, a transportation expert who had accompanied Ellershaw, remained in New York to assist the movement of completed supplies to Russia. Despite the new position, transportation difficulties would continue to plague the Russian supply effort.[42]

The cumulative effect of Kitchener's initiative to increase Russian supply orders abroad, however militarily sound, created a financial crisis for the British government, and subsequently for the Allies. The exchange value of the pound against the dollar had been slowly decreasing since December 1914, when it stood at $4.86. In June, Morgan had tested the waters for a major British loan issue and found that the market was not good. On July 20, Morgan informed the British that it could not purchase more dollars without driving the exchange rate to below $4.77, a new low, yet the constant flow of contracts demanded exchange. Two days later, the British government failed to complete a contract entered into for the Russians due to a lack of dollars. Morgan arranged a short-term loan guaranteed by British-owned American securities, but by August 14 the exchange rate had dropped to $4.70¼ and Morgan held only $4 million to pay $17 million in contracts due the next week. The prospect of a British government default was real and immediate.[43] Surveying the British position, a Treasury official wrote that "as regards September payments we shall be very hard put to ... meet existing commitments and any considerable addition to September cash liabilities ... will make debacle inevitable."[44] At the same time, however, the Russians were in the market for an additional £30 million in supplies.[45]

In response to the crisis, the British and French finance ministers held a conference in Boulogne, France, on August 20, 1915. The British presented their case that preservation of the exchange rate was more critical than the backing of national currencies. The French concurred, and both governments agreed to hold $200 million in gold each to be shipped to the United States if and when the Bank of England decided it was required. The Russian government was to be asked to contribute a like amount.[46]

The Russian finance minister, Bark, was unable to attend any Allied conference until late September.[47] Until then, he proposed the shipment of £40 million in gold to the United States in exchange for £400 million in credits. The British counter-offered £30 million in credits, but nothing further until after a conference. When Bark arrived in Britain, he found the British position on gold unyielding. Shipping Russian gold to allow Russia to pay its own debts contributed nothing to the overall Allied effort. The Anglo-French conference had envisioned a joint credit pool each ally could tap according to its contribution, based on a strong British pound. If Russia were to enjoy the benefits of Allied credits using the pound, it would have to pay to defend the exchange rate.[48]

The agreement signed between Britain and Russia on September 30, 1915, represented a Russian concession to British financial concerns.

Russia would hold £40 million in gold ready to back Allied, in place of exclusively Russian, purchases in the United States. The gold would be converted into British bonds payable in gold, salving Russian sensibilities with the idea that the gold was merely loaned from the Russian treasury. Britain extended to Russia a credit of £25 million per month for as long as the next twelve months, guaranteed by Russian Treasury notes. The funding of the second six months of the deal was made contingent on the British ability to secure financing in the United States, in part to provide a direct Russian stake in the stability of the pound sterling. The funds could be used for financing contracts placed already in Britain, North America, and, with limitations, Japan, servicing debt held anywhere other than France, and up to £45 million in new orders each month.[49]

More significant than the financial arrangements, however, was the annex to the agreement which attempted to bring order to Russian purchasing in the United States. After the rejection at the February Paris Conference, the British did not reiterate their proposal that J. P. Morgan and Company handle all Russian purchasing. They did, however, stipulate through the September agreement that all purchases financed with British money, either in Britain or North America, had to be approved by a committee of Russian representatives in London. The committee was to work with the British members of the Russian Purchasing Committee when ordering war materials and with the *Commission Internationale de Ravitaillement* on all other orders.[50] Further, the Russian representative in London was to be given authority to sign contracts binding the Russian government which previously required approval from the Russian War Ministry.[51] Finally, an annex to the agreement stipulated the formation of a formal Russian purchasing committee in America. Through the agreement, the British government hoped to force order on the Russian purchasing system.

That Bark had signed such an annex was perhaps due to the realization that effective control of purchasing would ultimately be in Russia's interest. Bark had received a rather nasty shock in July when he discovered that 380 million rubles in munitions orders had been placed in America without his ministry's knowledge.[52] Worse, as he confided to the British ambassador, one quarter of the sum, 95 million rubles, was due immediately as advances.[53] The Russian purchasing agents in America were doing their best to meet the shell crisis and were bound to bankrupt Russia in the process.

The sudden limitation of Russian foreign supply expenditure, while essential to the overall war effort, resulted in increased competition between the individual agencies of the Russian government. Each agency's requirements were now balanced against the requirements of other groups pursuing a finite amount of available money. The bureaucratic instinct was to eliminate competitors, and the state agencies moved to eliminate voluntary organizations from foreign purchasing. On November 16, 1915, the Council of Ministers resolved that "in the case of foreign market dealings, an appropriate organ must be formed directly by the government which does not depend on the cooperation of public-industrial organizations."[54] The phrase "public-industrial organizations" was aimed squarely at the War-Industries Committees, particularly the Central War-Industries Committee's Foreign Purchase Committee. Formed in August 1915 to order metals from abroad for its member factories, the committee had operated in competition with a special committee operated by the Ministry of Trade and Industry which was purchasing metal abroad for the government. The Foreign Purchase Committee initially attempted to skirt the order, redefining its functions as advisory in place of executive. Eventually, the minister of trade and industry demanded that the committee become a state organ. Interestingly, Finance Minister Bark joined in this demand, voicing the British government's approval for the move.[55]

As the officer in charge of financing Russia's war orders, Bark was acutely aware of the continued disorder in foreign purchasing. Excluding non-government actors from the foreign purchasing scene would reduce the number of agencies competing for supplies and funding, but it was the unplanned obligation of funds by other ministries that threatened to disrupt the tenuous flow of foreign exchange and supplies. While no minister could impose financial discipline on his counterparts, the September agreement held the promise that the combined efforts of British and Russian agents in America could impose order at the source.

3

A Committee in Earnest

The British frustrations that gave rise to the September 30 agreement were legion, and were best stated in an unusually candid letter Colonel Ellershaw sent to Stettinius in November 1915. Ellershaw, who had been working as Kitchener's action officer on the Russian supply problem for at least eight months at the time, sought to convince Stettinius, as the head of Allied purchasing for Morgan, of the continuing need to rein in the Russians. For Ellershaw, the acid test of purchasing was the successful completion and delivery of munitions. As for Russian sensibilities, Ellershaw believed that Britain needed to:

> accept the fact that whoever is at fault [for failure to deliver munitions], it is the British Government who will be blamed for all delays.... If we produce the stuff to time all will be forgiven by the Russian Government, if we do not, no excuse will be listened to.[1]

Ellershaw indicated that he had spent the past two months trying to insure that transport was planned for all orders placed in American. Despite his belief that "our duty in the matter is not finished until we have deposited the stuff on Russian soil," his efforts had come to naught. "As usual," he complained, "nothing has yet been done as the Russians have been unable to come to any decision as to who is to control arrangements." As for the new arrangement established by the September agreement, Ellershaw despaired of the London Committee asserting effective control over American purchasing. "General Hermonius," he observed, "is doing his honest best here [in London], but is very nervous of treading on the toes of Sapojnikov, and will not take a strong line." If the Russians could not police themselves, he concluded, the ultimate answer was for the British to exert more control over the supply system. "In my opinion," he wrote, "the days of 'the Velvet Glove' are over and the 'Mailed Fist' should be brought out."

Ellershaw's cynicism is perhaps more understandable when it is recalled that, in large part, the new arrangements did little more than formalize many of the existing relationships in Russian supply. The September 30 agreement between the British and Russian finance ministers required that the Russian Government Committee in London approve all future Russian purchases in Britain and America. The committee was to work in concert with the War Office Russian Purchasing Committee and the *Commission Internationale de Ravitaillement*. Since the Russian Government Committee had nominally exercised this authority for the last year, however, the agreement broke little new ground.

More significant was the idea that a formal counterpart to the Russian Government Committee in London be established in America. Where the idea for a centralized Russian Supply Commission in America originated is not entirely clear. Undoubtedly, the disorder in Russian purchasing in American was so apparent that the idea had been considered in many circles since August 1914.

Yet even the establishment of the Russian Supply Commission in America was not a radical departure. The new head of the commission, General Sapojnikov, already had authority over orders placed in America on behalf of the War Ministry. What was new was the expanded authority he received over non-military war orders. His new commission included the existing purchasing authorities of the *Glavnoe Artilleriiskoe Upravlenie*, the *Glavnoe Tekhnicheskoe Upravlenie* (Chief Technical Directorate), and the Military-Medical Authority, among others. By forcing these efforts under one authority, the British clearly hoped that better coordination and more rational procedures would result.

The new commission held its first meeting on October 13, 1915, in the Flatiron Building in New York City. In attendance were General Sapojnikov, Colonel Golevskii, and representatives of the Chief Technical Directorate, the Ministries of the Navy, Finance, Trade and Supply, the Central and Moscow War-Industries Committees, and the

All-Russian Zemstvo and Towns Union. At least in the official record, Sapojnikov made it clear that the commission was chartered strictly to act as an agent for the Russian Government Committee in London. According to a telegram read by General Sapojnikov to the members, "from this moment, not one contract can be closed by the committee in America without the knowledge and consent of the London Committee." Sapojnikov then mentioned that, based on a letter from the chairman of the All-Russian Unions of Zemstvos and Towns, and with the consent of the war minister, the two zemstvo representatives present were admitted as members.[2]

The presence of these representatives of Russian civil society in a government supply commission was perhaps the most extraordinary element of the newly formed committee. Educated, often in technical fields, and closely associated with liberal causes, these men provided a strong contrast to the military officers around them. The representative of the Central War-Industries Committee, Professor Boris Aleksandrovich Bakhmeteff, was probably the most colorful and influential example of the Russian liberal element in America during this era. Born in Tbilisi in 1880, Bakhmeteff was trained as an engineer at the Institute of the Ministry of Ways and Communications. Shortly after graduation he had come to the United States to work on the New York State Barge Canal. Returning to Russia in 1907, he earned a doctorate in engineering from the Polytechnic Institute in St. Petersburg in 1911 and served as a professor there before the war.[3]

At the time of the Russian Supply Commission's first meeting, Bakhmeteff was newly arrived in the United States, and General Sapojnikov used the opportunity both to introduce and query him. After a glowing introduction, Sapojnikov asked that, as most of the members of the commission had been in America for some time, Bakhmeteff explain to them the role and authority of the Special Committee for the Discussion and Coordination of Measures for the National Defense. Bakhmeteff obliged, explaining that the Special Committee was "the highest ranking organ dealing with questions of military supply" and listing its various members.[4]

It seems extraordinary that the senior Russian officer in the United States dealing with military supplies would be unfamiliar with the Special Committee. In the case of the Special Committee, as with so many Russian wartime organs, there was a gap between formal and actual authority.[5] Perhaps Sapojnikov, in questioning Bakhmeteff, was trying to discern the actual influence of the new body. Regardless, the inquiry speaks to the difficulties in information flow that plagued Russian efforts.

Sapojnikov had good reason to care about the attitude of the Special Committee. Under the new unified purchasing arrangement, the Special Committee represented the ultimate authority in Petrograd dealing with international supply. On November 19, 1915, this committee would formally authorize the regulations governing the Russian Supply Commission in America. The committee, itself a joint state Duma–society arrangement, formally stipulated in the regulations that the American commission include representatives of the All-Russian Unions of Zemstvos and Towns and the Central War-Industries Committee.[6]

At the second meeting of the Russian Supply Commission in America, the question of committee assignments for the three newly arrived Central War-Industries Committee representatives arose. Sapojnikov addressed the commission, saying that:

> Undoubtedly, the very fact that the formation of the Russian Supply Commission in America included representatives of the social organs shows a response to social events, occurring now in Russia, where it is observed that there is more and more unity between the representatives of government authority and society.[7]

Thus, the general concluded "we can sincerely welcome into organizational activity on contracts in America our new members from two recognized points of view."[8]

While in some way endorsed by their inclusion in the Russian Supply Commission, the American purchasing efforts of the All-Russian Unions of Zemstvos and Towns and the Central War-Industries Committee betrayed their rather haphazard origins. The zemstvo effort had begun with the arrival of Alexander Sakhnovsky in the United States, probably in early 1915. The son of a Smolensk land owner, Sakhnovsky's father Nicholas had been a member of the zemstvo delegation that had greeted Nicholas II on his ascension to the throne and been rebuffed for their petition. Active in peacetime zemstvo work, shortly after the war began Alexander was commissioned by Prince Lvov to take charge of zemstvo shoe purchasing in Russia. An American importer offered shoes, but at a high price. Unsuccessful in the search for raw materials at home, he responded by leading a delegation to the United States to buy shoes. Once in America, he was besieged with cables from other zemstvo elements requesting help acquiring other items, and by default became the zemstvo purchasing representative in America.[9]

For all the work of the zemstvo and industrial representatives, it was the more colorful unofficial efforts that received the most play in the press. One notorious example began in November 1915, when Nicholas Riabouchinsky arrived in New York with his wife, described as "a noted Italian beauty," and fifteen trunks of artwork. A former Russian diplomat, Riabouchinsky claimed to represent an unnamed Moscow war committee seeking to sell $1 million worth of artwork to raise money for the war effort. Riabouchinsky was eventually forced to deny publicly any ties to the Russian government or the Central War-Industries Committee. He remained in the United States as a business representative and made the press in connection with his alleged gambling debts and eventual divorce.[10]

Even as the zemstvo representatives were being warmly integrated into the Russian Supply Commission, the efforts of the union were raising increased suspicions among elements of the Imperial government. For conservatives within the government, such suspicions were nothing new. In response to a November 1914 request for a congress of voluntary associations, Interior Minister Maklakov replied:

> I cannot give you permission for convening such a congress; it would be an undesirable and universal demonstration to the effect that there exist disorders in supplying the army. Besides, I do not wish to give permission, since under the guise of delivering boots, you will begin to make a revolution.[11]

The union was dominated by liberal political officials, mostly Kadets, and was heavily influenced by former Moscow officials. A number of these officials, Prince Lvov among them, had been key in the Moscow City Council's continual attempts after the 1905 Revolution to exploit the government's concessions as much as possible. Lvov had been nominated as mayor of Moscow in 1913 only to have the minister of the interior refuse to approve his taking office.[12]

The Russian government was increasingly unhappy with the tone of the "progressive" elements in domestic politics, but it was also aware that the traditional liberal parties, particularly the Constitutional Democrats, had strong links to liberal elements abroad. In a coalition warfare environment, the government was forced to consider how its Allies abroad would perceive its actions. During August at least two prominent liberals expressed the opinion that only the foreign minister's planned visit to Britain was delaying the Tsar's order to prorogue the Duma sitting scheduled for September 3.[13]

The Inter-Allied Munitions Conference opened in London on November 23, 1915. Hosted by Lloyd George, Russian interests were represented by the Admiral A. I. Rusin, who lodged extravagant demands for the coming year.[14] Rusin's presentation, combined with the Russian's systematic violations of the September 30 agreement, continued the erosion of British confidence in their ally. In British eyes, even Bark, who certainly understood the need for coordination and limits in supply matters, often seemed to regard the September agreement as statement of common goals rather than a strictly observed agreement. For the Russians, acutely aware of the price their nation was paying in blood for the Allied cause, any comment that seemed to reduce the rarefied goals of the alliance to simple commercial paper was an insult to the national honor.

The issue of railway equipment proved a continuing irritation to both parties. On April 6, 1916, A. F. Trepov, the Russian minister of ways and communications, submitted to the British government an urgent request for £12 million in rolling stock. The ministry deemed the new cars necessary for the coming summer offensive and desired to negotiate the purchase independent of British control. By June the British Treasury replied that the requested amount of supplies likely exceeded the transport that the Russians had available. At most, they suggested, the Russians might ship £5 million in goods, but that, in any event, all allotted Russian credits had been expended on previous orders. "It is probable," Treasury warned, "that Their Lordships will be forced by financial considerations to adopt the policy that no more orders of any kind must be placed in America except in quite exceptional circumstances."[15] In June, Bark made inquiries of both British and French financial houses seeking funding for Russian railroads. The Russian government sought some 585 million rubles for existing uncompleted roads, 152 million rubles in improvements to completed roads and 166 million rubles in new orders with no success.[16]

Despite the strong warning, the Russians continued their ongoing negotiations for railroad supplies. When the British Treasury testily pointed out that the Russians could rely on neither British financial nor transportation aid for these orders, the Russian reply was simple and disingenuous. American suppliers had demanded immediate commitments, and as the railroad supplies were essential to the war, the Russians felt they had no alternative but to place the orders.[17]

By spring 1916, it was clear to the British that the September agreement had failed to organize Russia purchasing efforts in America. Visits by General Hermonius had produced temporary improvements in the relations between the Russian Supply Commission in America and its British counterparts and American suppliers but no lasting reform. After gaining approval from Petrograd, Kitchener ordered the newly promoted Brigadier General Ellershaw to America as the permanent British War Office representative to the Russian Supply Commission in America. Ellershaw's travels to Russia on behalf of Lord Kitchener had made him known to both the War Ministry and the *Stavka*. Trusted by Kitchener, experienced in dealing with Russians, and involved in Russian supply issues since the beginning of the war, Ellershaw was the ideal British representative.[18]

Before he could embark on the task of repairing Russian supply in the United States, Ellershaw was required to perform one more task on behalf of his superior. Anglo-Russian supply issues had been a military concern of Lord Kitchener since fall 1914, and there is every evidence that he took his May 1915 charge from Grand Duke Nicholas as a personal responsibility. On May 13, 1916, the Russian ambassador had conveyed to Kitchener the tsar's personal invitation to travel to Russia. There he could visit the front and gain first-hand knowledge of the Russian supply situation. Kitchener accepted and planned his arrival in Arkhangel'sk for June 9 and Petrograd for June 11, carefully permitting himself several days to confer with Russian Finance Minister Bark before Bark was required to depart for the June Allied Conference in Paris. On June 5, Kitchener, Ellershaw, and a small staff, embarked the cruiser H.M.S. *Hampshire*. Some two hours out of Scapa Flow, *Hampshire* struck a German submarine-laid mine and sank in less than fifteen minutes. As *Hampshire's* escorting destroyers had been detached due to the heavy weather, only thirteen aboard survived their prolonged exposure to the cold of the North Sea. Kitchener and Ellershaw were not among them.[19]

While mourned in both Britain and Russia, Kitchener's arbitrary leadership style and tendency to operate outside of recognized channels probably made his death something of a relief to the British purchasing bureaucracy. The loss of Ellershaw, however, had an immediate effect on British plans to improve the purchasing situation in America. The Russian supply situation demanded immediate attention, and the Ministry of Munitions moved quickly to find Ellershaw's replacement.

Less than ten days after the sinking, Lloyd George, minister of munitions, cabled General F. F. Minchin to propose that he assume Ellershaw's portfolio to repair Russian purchasing. Minchin had served as the head of munitions inspection in Great Britain until being sent to New York in April to improve the British inspection effort in America. Lloyd George acknowledged that these reorganization efforts on the British side were going well, and it is clear from the tone of Lloyd George's cable that he was offering Minchin a difficult and possibly unwelcome assignment. "I feel strongly," he wrote, "that the allied cause would be most effectively served by your taking up the duties ... which it was General Ellershaw's intention to fulfill in America." But Minchin needed to be warned that the ministry:

> was not able to obtain unequivocal powers for General Ellershaw in writing, and without a doubt the same state of affairs would exist if you were appointed; but I am convinced that by the judicious use of your personal influence and experience, and with the aid of your military repute, these difficulties with inspection would be overcome.[20]

After consulting with Stettinius, Minchin agreed to the appointment. Minchin would come to be widely respected in American circles, despite lacking the experience and personal ties that Ellershaw would have brought to the task.

Bark, meanwhile, arrived safely for the June conference of Allied finance ministers in Paris. The conference was delayed from its planned June 26 opening as the ongoing Irish Easter Uprising detained British Finance Minister McKenna. Ultimately, after a delay of several weeks, the conference was moved to London so that McKenna could attend. There Bark presented his case for increased Allied financial support. In response, the British observed that the impending American presidential election would make any significant loans from the United States impossible until after November, limiting the credit available for Russian needs. Further, the British asserted that Russian transport limitations made new orders superfluous. In response, Colonel Beliaev presented statistics which purported to prove that shipping capacity and Russian ports could accommodate new orders, conspicuously ignoring the issue of internal rail transport. Bark wanted from the Allies an assurance that Russia's critical military needs, particularly heavy artillery, would be met regardless of any credit limitations. While Bark was generally unsatisfied with the tone and results of the conference, he did succeed in convincing the British to surge purchasing credits forward to meet what the Russians identified as critical needs.[21]

As a result of the ongoing transportation crisis, the Russians and British created the May 5, 1916 agreement "as to the necessary procedure to be established in order to ensure transport of munitions to Russia."[22] Signed by the British Admiralty and General Hermonius and endorsed by Grey and Benkendorf, the agreement was predicated on the Russian estimate that 2.6 million tons of stores could be shipped through the White Sea ports between May 1916 and May 1917. During this one-year period, the British agreed to provide shipping for some 2 million tons of stores, 250,000 tons of which was American munitions. The Admiralty also took responsibility to "sweep and mark a channel" to prevent loss due to mining or navigational hazard. In exchange, the Admiralty insisted on the right to appoint a Principal Naval Transport Officer (P.T.N.O.) in Arkhangel'sk as advisor to the port commander. The P.T.N.O. would have control over the loading of British vessels for their return voyages. They also insisted that the northern route be closed to any shipping without a special license "delivered by the Russia delegate in the International Supply Commission in London, in agreement with the British Admiralty."

On June 28, 1916, General Sapojnikov attended a meeting of the Transportation Committee at India House, Kingsway, in Britain, intended to address coordination of shipping between the Russian Supply Commissions in London and New York. The British representatives made it clear that they were prepared to ship supplies other than those ordered through J. P. Morgan and Company, provided that the Morgan orders were loaded first and the total tonnage for the year did not exceed the 250,000 allotted in May.

The true limiting factor in Russian overseas supply was not ocean shipping. Rather, effective use of imports was dependent on the thin line of transportation from the ports to the inland areas. Goods delivered to Vladivostok in the east, usually after having transshipped most of North America, faced the single, speed- and weight-limited track of the Trans-Siberian railway. Goods that made the torturous passage to the Murman Coast had even more limited options. The primary Russian port, Arkhangel'sk, was served by a single narrow gauge rail line, which resulted in tremendous backlogs of stores. While the closure of the port each year during the late winter offered the opportunity to clear out the accumulation, the excess continued to grow. The British military attaché observed that most of the delayed stores were left unprotected in the open. In 1915, the Russians were working to expand the line to standard gauge in the expectation of having the modification done by 1916.[23] As with so many Russian estimates, this goal was not met.

The Allies desperately wanted to avoid the White Sea closure by using the warm water ports of the western Murman Coast or Norway. Throughout the war, the British government pressured Sweden to permit the passage of supplies to Russia, and some limited shipments were made. Sweden, however, was officially neutral and temperamentally anti-Russian; and until 1916, British pressure was tempered by fear of Swedish belligerency against Russia. The overextended Russians could scarce afford another front.[24] In desperation, the British government financed a three-hundred-mile sled route from Skibotten to the northern terminus of the Finnish rail system. The limited hauling ability of the line and losses due probable to German sabotage led it to be considered a failure. More promising was the effort to build a seven hundred-mile railway from the ice-free Kola Inlet to the northern terminus of the Russian rail system. The Russian Council of Ministers had funded the effort in December 1914, and construction on each of the three major sections began in 1915. The construction faced daunting challenges, ranging from Arctic weather to miles of swamp requiring bridging to a complete absence of locally available labor and supplies. The line was eventually opened on November 28, 1916, too late to impact the Imperial war effort.[25]

The British government was acutely aware of this tenuous network and had initially made the 1916 Admiralty shipping agreement contingent on "the arrangements for clearing the ships at Archangel proving prompt and satisfactory."[26] The closure of the Russian northern ports to all but licensed vessels in the final agreement represented a British effort to force the Russians to maintain the agreed upon priorities for shipments. With limited transport, the Russian habit of shipping non-essential goods or delaying Allied munitions shipments in favor of other items was, in the British view, injurious to the war effort.

One means to discourage Russian orders outside of British control was to increase the expense of shipping them. The Anglo-Russian agreement on shipping rates from American to the White Sea for 1916 divided cargoes into three categories; "Morgan orders," "Russian orders," and "private orders." "Morgan orders" were British government orders placed through J. P. Morgan and Company. "Russian orders" were orders placed by the Russian Supply Commission, while "private orders" were war materials approved for shipment by the committee. The first two types of cargo enjoyed the subsidized rate of 65s. per ton, while private orders were charged "not less than $30 per ton." [27]

With transportation problems, ongoing problems with Russian inspections were a key factor in the establishment of the Russian Supply Commission in America. Within the Russian Supply Commission in America, inspections fell under the authority of the *Glavnoe Tekhnicheskoe Upravlenie*, or Chief Technical Directorate. Each area of production had an independent chief inspector who nominally reported to the Technical Directorate. A Morgan representative, however, commented that:

> While the Russian Technical Bureau is presumably in charge of all inspections, it appears to exercise little control over the inspectors and their

> assistants, and appeals from decisions of inspectors are said to receive little if any consideration under the present arrangement.[28]

American manufacturers found that there was no one inspector in charge of all the inspections at their factory. Instead, a manufacturer would have to deal with a number of assistant inspectors, each responsible for a single component of the finished product. Thus a manufacturer of artillery shells would be forced to refer to separate assistant inspectors in charge of shell casings, fuzes, primers and so on. Each assistant inspector would report independently to a chief inspector in charge of that particular item. This chief inspector was responsible for the technical inspection of his one assigned component at each manufacturer in the United States. As if this division was not difficulty enough, a Morgan representative observed that the many of the assistant inspectors were "inexperienced in munitions of any kind" and that few spoke English.[29] From his post in Petrograd, General Knox, the British military attaché, could discern:

> The Artillery Department was in the habit of sending men abroad as inspectors, who were without any technical knowledge, and were therefore obliged to follow the specifications pedantically and without intelligence. On one occasion an officer told me his brother had gone to England to "take over" big guns. I asked if he knew anything of gunnery. The reply was: "No. He is a lawyer by education, an artist by inclination, and a cavalry officer by occupation."[30]

As a result, the assistant inspectors deferred significant decisions to their chief, who was often on the road visiting one of the dozens of plants where his component was being made. Since each chief inspector interpreted the standards himself and the Technical Bureau was loath to overrule these officials, one chief inspector could create a production bottleneck across the United States by rejecting key components. Difficulties with inspections were a recurring theme with American manufacturers, and contributed significantly to production delays. In an internal memorandum written after the war, J. P. Morgan and Company highlighted their problems with Russian inspections:

> The experience with Russian contracts for complete artillery ammunition afforded sharp contrast [with those of the British]. There was difficulty with the drawings and designs from the outset. Frequent and arbitrary changes were made. No assistance was available from a suitable government production organization, and the inspection of the Russian Mission was

> unsympathetic and sometimes even hostile. The result was frequent delays, unsatisfactory product, and eventually a partial cancellation.[31]

The contrast between British and Russian inspections is more striking when it is recalled that the British government confronted the same production challenges that stymied the Russians. The British inspection staff, however, took the view that, in addition to actual inspection, their job included doing "whatever was possible to help the firms to ... make the largest possible deliveries...." Responsibility for British inspections was divided among three chief inspectors, each responsible for a geographic region rather than a type of product. In April 1916, when General F. F. Minchin arrived in the United States to reorganize and improve British inspection, he further decentralized the inspections process, dividing the three regions into six, and established a system of sub-regions. The British were also willing to employ non–British citizens in inspection work and professed to be pleased with the results. By 1916, British government inspections employed more than 2,400 personnel, of whom only 150 had come from England.[32]

The experience of the Westinghouse Company was not untypical. Despite holding the two largest rifle contracts the Russians placed in the United States, Westinghouse was unable to acquire a set of Russian gauges that could be used as a standard for the acceptance of rifles. Lacking this basic equipment, the company manufactured its own gauges and proceeded with the contract. Some months later, a partial set of Russian gauges arrived. These Russian gauges had been in use in Russia since 1892, and as a result of wear matched neither the American manufactured gauges nor the technical drawings that the Russian government had provided. The senior Russian inspectors, while freely admitting that the Russian gauges were defective, made it clear that Westinghouse deviated from the gauges at its own risk. In an attempt to end this impasse, the Russian government sent forty Russian manufactured rifles to serve as a guide in the event of uncertainty. The Russian inspectors at Westinghouse declined to accept these rifles as authoritative—despite direction to do so—as they were wartime production rifles and, by inference, made to less exacting tolerances.

In some cases, Russian inspectors did not trust the production of other Westinghouse plants and would only approve rifles where each component was manufactured in their plant. Thus, while Westinghouse's plant in East Springfield could produce sufficient rifle stocks for it and several other plants, the plant in Meridian produced its own stocks in order to satisfy the Russian inspectors in Meridian. As a result, the failure of the equipment necessary to produce a given part at any plant could delay the entire production of rifles from that plant, as the Russian inspectors would not permit the shifting of interchangeable components from another plant.[33]

The intractability of the Russian inspectors placed the British in an unenviable position. While the Russians were responsible for the technical side of the contracts, including the inspection and acceptance of the supplies, the contracts were legally between the American companies and His Britannic Majesty's government. While the contracts typically offered an arbitration clause, General Minchin pointed out that "if the arbitration which is mentioned in the contracts is called into effect, it will be arbitration between the contractors and the British Government."[34] The British government, dependent on the good graces of the American markets, was not in a position to pursue aggressively claims against major American companies, yet their failure to do so would surely aggravate relations with the Russians.

The British government examined three options for the resolution of the inspections issue. The first, maintaining the status quo, was fundamentally untenable. The inefficiencies and aggravations of the Russian inspectors were choking off vital supplies and destroying Allied goodwill with American industrialists. The second, and most radical, was to remove inspection authority from the Russian Supply Commission in America and rely on British inspections. While favored by Lloyd George, the ever prickly Russian delegations could hardly be expected to accede to such an action quietly, and there remained questions as to British ability to supply enough technical personnel for the task. The third, compromise position, was the formation of a joint British and Russian Committee to control orders and inspections.[35]

By June, drafts of a British proposal to establish a coordinating committee between the British and Russian purchasing representatives in America were circulating between London and New York. In the course of these discussions, it was evident that a number of officials, Russian, British and American, had concluded that a significant problem in the Russian Supply Commission in America was its leader, General Sapojnikov. In June, a Morgan representative in London observed to Stettinius that the root problem in America was that Sapojnikov and his mission:

> went out to America chiefly as a purchasing commission and on account of arrangements whereby a large proportion of Russian Government purchases was undertaken by [the] British government

> the Commission ... found themselves to a certain extent superseded and ... felt a considerable amount of soreness over the whole matter.[36]

Informally, the British had already been assured that Sapojnikov would be replaced. Sapojnikov, who was visiting London for a planned Anglo-Russian conference in July, would return to the United States only to introduce his replacement. In fact, the Morgan representative reported, "efforts are being made to avoid [the] necessity of Maj. Gen. Sapojnikov returning to [the] United States, even temporarily...."[37]

General Sapojnikov's proposed replacement, Lieutenant-General Zaluboffsky, was already in London, working with the Supply Commission there. The Morgan representative reported approvingly that Zaluboffsky was "a highly experienced technical and practical man ... and has already been very helpful in straightening out inspection difficulties under Russian contracts in [Britain]."[38] Members of his staff in the United States would eventually regard him as "a cruel man" and comment on his close connections to the War Ministry bureaucracy.[39]

As the prospective president of the Russian Supply Commission in America, Zaluboffsky was asked to comment on the British proposal for an Anglo-Russian Sub-Committee. The British had initially proposed that all decisions of the sub-committee be required to be unanimous. General Hermonius had objected to this clause earlier, proposing that:

> In the absence of a unanimous decision in connection with difficulties arising on questions of inspection, the President of the Russian Supply Committee (American) shall, with the concurrence of the Contractors have the right to amend the Conditions of inspection....

U. F. Wintour, the director of army contracts, negotiating for the British, had rejected this change. Zaluboffsky restated the Russian position that technical issues, including inspection issues, should not require a unanimous decision:

> It is quite evident that if a unanimous decision of the Anglo-Russian Sub-Committee is insisted upon to decide every misunderstanding in connection with inspection ... it would be impossible to avoid delaying such decisions....[40]

What, he asked hypothetically, would happen if he as president of the commission were visiting a munitions contractor and became aware of an inspection problem? Rather than being able to issue authoritative guidance on the spot, he would be required to return to New York and seek concurrence from the Anglo-Russian Sub-Committee. "Such a state of affairs would," he suggested, not only "...paralyse the activity of the President, but would be in direct contradiction with ... the acceleration of deliveries...." Zaluboffsky emphasized that his object was not to gain control over British financial commitments:

> In so far as the British Government may have financed a particular Russian order, that Government is naturally entitled to a wide and strict control over the carrying out of such an order. On my part, I not only have nothing against such a control—I emphatically welcome it!

But, he continued, the Russian government also had a right to insure that its forces were supplied with goods that met its standards.

The British were clearly uncomfortable with not exercising veto authority over all decisions primarily because they feared an exemption for "technical" questions would be stretched by the Russians to encompass a variety of controversies. As a compromise, Zaluboffsky proposed a seemingly straightforward set of definitions. "Technical questions" would involve inspection of supplies and entail no additional expenditure on the part of the British. Issues involving any new British expenditure would be considered "financial questions" even if inspection was also involved. The Russian president would decide technical questions, while the British representative would decide financial issues.

As negotiations progressed, the Morgan office in London sought to provide Stettinius with insight into the thinking behind the British position. Commenting on an early draft, the Morgan office noted that while the bulk of the agreement dealt with the placement of new orders, the British government considered it "unlikely that the Russian Government will be able to place any important amount of fresh orders in [the] United States." For the few new orders that would be placed, British financial control allowed them "to dictate the terms on which these shall be arranged." This knowledge allowed the British negotiators to create an agreement on new orders "and endeavor to work into it necessary arrangements regarding inspection and administration of existing contracts." Thus, "the real importance of the agreement is considered to lie ... in clause six" because "only clause six bears directly upon the administration and inspection of existing contracts."[41]

General Minchin, through Morgan Company channels, was provided with this analysis and was asked to comment on the draft agreement. Minchin pointed out that, whatever the description of the committee's official role, the execution of its decision would "remain in the hands of [a] body of inspectors who in the past have shown themselves independent of control and ... have ignored written decisions of General Hermonius himself." The proposed arrangement, he concluded, was "at best only palliative."[42]

In their commentary, Stettinius and Minchin strongly recommended that the British government request that the new sub-committee include Professor Bakhmeteff. While they were aware that the British recommending a Russian, particularly a non-governmental representative, to sit for the Russians was rife with potential political problems, they clearly valued his practical expertise. Bakhmeteff, they offered, had worked well with the American contractors, was familiar with business and manufacturing conditions in America and spoke English well.[43]

The agreement that established the Anglo-Russian Sub-Committee as part of the Russian Supply Commission in America was finalized during the Anglo-Russian Conference held July 13–16, 1916, in London and Grey and Benkendorf formally signed on July 14. The agreement granted Russian inspectors "complete freedom of action" in dealing with "questions of a purely technical nature." However, questions that involved "the financial liability" of the British government—not merely additional expenditures—were to be decided by unanimous vote of the sub-committee. In total, the agreement represented a loss of influence for the Russian Supply Commission in America. At the same time, the death of Lord Kitchener had removed Russian supply issues from the special protection of the War Office and the Russian Purchasing Committee was officially transferred to the Ministry of Munitions.[44]

Despite British efforts, General Sapojnikov did return to the United States for a brief time following the conference. In a July meeting of the commission, he made it clear that he did not view the trip to Britain as a failure. As he recounted with evident pride to the members, he had been received by King George V of Britain and invested with the order of Knight Commander of Saints Michael and George.[45]

4

The Russian-British Axis Cemented

The Anglo-Russian Sub-Committee, created by agreement between Grey and Benkendorf at the July Conference in London, was the last great attempt to place Russian orders in the United States on a rational footing. Of course, for the Russian Supply Commission in America, the Anglo-Russian Sub-Committee was an outside imposition, not organic to the structure of the commission. However comprehensive the agreement signed in London attempted to be, the exigencies of the war would undoubtedly require improvisation to meet supply needs. Further, the British had yet to produce a document whose intent the Russians could not effectively stymie. The success or failure of the effort hinged on how the Russians in New York would deal with the new committee.

The reason for the sub-committee's existence was two-fold. It was first to bring order to the placement of new British-funded orders in America. Second, it was to address the lack of results from the contracts already placed with American firms. Addressing the failure of existing contracts meant dealing with the persistent complaints from American manufacturers about dealing with Russian inspectors. Even granting that these complaints typically came from firms that were unable to meet their agreed delivery dates, the extent of the problem was daunting.

The British representatives in the Anglo-Russian Sub-Committee were acutely aware of the failures of the Russian inspection system. The massive Russian contract with Eddystone Ammunition Corporation was facing delays, and the corporation insisted that these problems were due to "changes in design and inefficient or inadequate inspection." On August 17, 1916, the British used the sub-committee to gather, in addition to the usual representatives of the British and Russian supply commissions, representatives of the Russian Chief Artillery Directorate, the chief Russian inspectors at Eddystone, officers of the Eddystone Corporation and Stettinius, representing J. P. Morgan and Company. Such a meeting ought have been a key opportunity to resolve these inspection problems. From the tone of the minutes, however, it appears that the meeting instead focused on the question of blame. The Russians conceded that "a certain amount of delay may have arisen from the beforementioned causes." However, "such delay was inseparable from the usual difficulties encountered in starting a new industry on a large scale." Certainly no change in the current Russian inspection system was required.[1]

The British would try again on October 3, 1916, when the issue of inspection at the Westinghouse Electric Company was addressed. Westinghouse held a large contract for the manufacture of Russian pattern rifles, and, like Eddystone, alleged that Russian inspection procedures were delaying completion of the contract. The sub-committee, which had been created largely to alleviate such problems, dodged the issue, pointing out to the representatives of Westinghouse present that:

> matters dealing with inspection were under the control of General Khrabroff, as President of the Artillery Commission, and that any suggested changes in inspection matters should be taken up by the Company direct with General Khrabroff.

Of course, General Khrabroff, as was his habit, was sitting in the meeting. It was clear that the Russians were not willing to discuss their inspection issues in a joint British-Russian venue. While the sub-committee did offer to entertain revised delivery schedules and even direct financial assistance to Westinghouse, it would once again provide no relief from the Russian inspections that were a major cause of the problem at hand.[2]

In appointing General Minchin as the senior British representative to the Anglo-Russian Sub-Committee, the British had shown the importance they placed on the inspection question. As the head of British inspection efforts in America, Minchin was a well-regarded player in munitions supply.[3] After General Ellershaw's untimely death in June, Minchin had inherited responsibility for Russian coordination while simultaneously continuing as head of British inspection in the United States. Minchin was painfully aware of how jealously the Russian delegation defended its inspection prerogatives and within the sub-committee his suggestions to improve the situation were typically phrased in careful, diplomatic terms. His control over British inspections gave him the resources to offer the Russians technical advice and substantive assistance. Thus, at the sub-committee's second meeting, when the discussion turned to the Canadian Car and Foundry Company orders, the British representatives could suggest "that the Production Engineers of the British Munitions Department should be made use of as occasion demanded in conjunction with men designated by the Imperial Russian Supply Committee." With ultimate control remaining in their hands, the Russians accepted the offer of British assistance.[4]

The Canadian Car and Foundry Company orders were naturally a central issue for the newly formed sub-committee. By March 1915, the firm had Russian orders for 5 million urgently needed shells worth $82 million, with delivery scheduled to commence in August 1915. With no experience in munitions orders, the firm grossly underestimated the difficulties of shell production. By late 1915, the Russian orders had destroyed the company's financial health to the point that bankruptcy was a possibility. When Canadian Car finally did deliver its first shells in December 1915, the company president took the opportunity to provide the British government, in the person of Colonel Ellershaw, with a revised schedule of deliveries and a request for additional funds. The British considered the schedule completely unrealistic, and questioned the company's ability to provide security for an advance. The Russian Supply Commission in America, reflecting the Russian ire at a year of failed deliveries, offered limited aid in exchange for major changes in the existing contracts. The Russian orders were to be entrusted to a separate company formed expressly for the purpose. At Russian insistence, the new contracts included stringent penalty clauses, which prompted the company to revise once again its schedule of deliveries.[5]

Despite these efforts, Canadian Car continued to fail to meet its production requirements.[6] One of the first orders of business for the Anglo-Russian Sub-Committee was the question of what approach to take to the company. Essentially, the question before the committee was whether to enforce the penalty clauses against the firm, forcing the British government into court and the company ultimately into bankruptcy, or to nurse the company along, hoping to ultimately receive some return on the investment. On August 4, 1916, the sub-committee "agreed that the Agency of the Canadian Car & Foundry Company must be saved from Bankruptcy and assisted to complete its contracts without financial loss." Toward that end, the sub-committee approved a total of $2,555,292.52 in immediate loans to the company.[7]

Two meetings later, the sub-committee took up a proposal for a revised contract with Canadian Car. Part of the new agreement included a revision of the financial penalties due under the original contract. By the first agreement, Canadian Car owed some $8.25 million because of its failure to deliver shells on time. The sub-committee discussed $2 million, and eventually settled on $3.5 million in penalties and interest as their offer to the company.[8]

The real contention occurred over the funding of the company. With the new contract, Canadian Car had requested an additional loan of $3,855,878.25. The Russian and British members disagreed over the wisdom of such an advance. The Russians pointed out that during the previous three weeks the company had received almost $4.3 million in loans and could offer only $7.25 million in securities. The total amount of loans and advances given the company well exceeded the value of the company's securities. The British members believed that "to encourage deliveries it was essential that the Company be provided with necessary money." Further, they reminded the Russians that they were in the habit of not disbursing the entire amount of approved loans, which forced the company to return to request more funds. The Russians retorted that "the handling of the loans was the only means of controlling the Company ... in the opinion of the Russian members, it was dangerous to finance the Company profusely without ... having some other means of controlling its activity." The British argument that the company could be controlled without starving it of needed operating capital eventually carried the day, and a cable was sent to the British Treasury requesting the loan. However, the pattern for sub-committee dealings with Canadian Car had been established. The British members would argue for accommodation, while the Russians would counsel severity.[9]

In the midst of these multiple and inter-related crises the ineffective General Sapojnikov was finally removed. If J. P. Morgan and Company and the British government had already seen and approved of his replacement, Lieutenant General Zaluboffsky, the members of the Russian Supply Commission in America were less certain. When the newly formed Anglo-Russian Sub-Committee met for the first time on July 31, 1916, the meeting dealt with one outstanding contract and then dissolved into "a prolonged discussion as to the attitude of General Zaluboffsky, in regard to the power of the Sub-Committee." Since the new commander's intentions would define the power of the committee, the group adjourned until the meeting of the full Russian Supply Committee scheduled for the next day.[10]

Having had the benefit of spending several months attached to the London Committee, Zaluboffsky did indeed arrive in the United States with definite opinions as to the supply process in operation in the United States and the functions of the Anglo-Russian Sub-Committee. Zaluboffsky assumed command in late August 1916, and on August 25, delivered an extraordinarily blunt change of command speech to the commission.[11] He was appointed, he told his subordinates, because of "the considerable delay in execution of some of our orders placed with American firms." These delays, he believed, were caused by failures in the contracts themselves, as well as by failures in the technical management of the contracts. In the first case, companies had agreed to delivery dates that could not possibly be filled. Rather than engage in the usual recriminations and additional delays, Zaluboffsky stated that "this must be considered only as a matter of fact ... my duty [is] to ascertain the exact date of delivery...." As for technical failures, the general suggested that the commission "may have to make the conditions of inspection easier ... and even then, in gross production we will inevitably obtain deviations from the normal technical conditions."[12]

Beyond techniques, Zaluboffsky made it clear that the commission's problems were in part institutional:

> "While in Petrograd," I became fully convinced that neither the Special Council for the Defense of the Realm nor the separate War Office Departments nor the Foreign Exchange Commission are in possession of exact and incontestable data with regard to the orders placed in the United States. Therefore, all the calculations of the above mentioned offices are vague and indefinite.... The question of appropriating money to the American Committee for the payment of extant orders and the question of the distribution of new orders ... can not be satisfactorily settled in London and in Petrograd unless the American Committee will furnish exact and complete data concerning the number and the character of orders placed in the United States and concerning the amount of money already paid on those orders.[13]

Clearly the commission which was to organize American orders had failed in its task, and the new commander, at the least, realized it. One of his charges to the commission was "a way of registering all new orders" to provide a central record of commitments.

Zaluboffsky also directed the establishment of three new departments within the commission: legal, finance, and government control. He was not comfortable relying on the commission's American attorney as his only counsel and appointed a Russian lawyer as head of the new department with the American as his advisor. The Finance Department was created because the officer then administering financial issues had also recently been appointed military attaché to the United States. Either position represented a full-time job, and the department was an attempt to keep the financial situation from foundering.[14]

The state of disorder in Russian contracts is clearly demonstrated in Zaluboffsky's instructions to establish a Department of Government Control. At his direction, the signature of the officer in charge of the department "will be affixed to every document," a step that would "remove all misunderstandings and disputes in regard to the legality of expenditures ... assigned to the Committee." Such a department would have had the effect of forcing the non-governmental representatives to gain governmental approval of their orders.

In his change of command speech, General Zaluboffsky had addressed the British members of the Anglo-Russian Sub-Committee. The general offered the optimistic view that "in regard to supplying the armies there is no difference of opinion, in England nor in Russia which may lead to a controversy." While there were no disputes, "there may be misunderstandings arising from the ... insufficient knowledge of each other and ... of mutual needs and means."[15]

If there was any question among the members of the Russian Supply Commission that General Zaluboffsky had arrived under instruction to clean up affairs, at least one member of his entourage should have removed any doubt. The enigmatic Ensign Boris Lvovich Brasol arrived with General Zaluboffsky and was introduced as the legal advisor to the Anglo-Russian Sub-Committee. Brasol was a well-connected military prosecutor and former criminal prosecutor in Petrograd. Strongly interested in the emerging science of criminology, Brasol had been one of six prosecutors sent abroad before the war for advanced training, studying in Switzerland and Paris. With the coming of the war, Brasol received a commission as an ensign and became a military prosecutor. In 1915, he was selected as one of the prosecutors of the Minister of War, General Sukhomlinov.[16] In 1916, not long after the trial, his book *Methods of Criminal Investigation* was published in Petrograd. In it, he used the questioning of a munitions factory official conducted during the Sukhomlinov investigation as a case study in correct interrogation technique.[17] Prior to his departure for the United States, Brasol had been briefed by members of the Special Council on potential espionage and criminal problems with the Russian Supply Commission in America. While officially the legal advisor, Brasol in fact served as secretary to General Zaluboffsky and conducted confidential investigations of committee members.[18]

Also arriving with General Zaluboffsky was Professor A. I. Astroff, who became the senior zemstvo representative in America. With the new arrivals, there were shortly two prominent departures. General Zaluboffsky removed Colonel Golevskii, who had been part of the earliest supply efforts in America and returned him to Russia. Golevskii had been Sapojnikov's primary assistant, and it was clear Zaluboffsky believed he was partly to blame for the disorder in supply.

More ominous was the removal of Professor Bakhmeteff from his position as chief of the Central War-Industries Committee delegation. Sapojnikov had clearly permitted Bakhmeteff and his delegation great freedom in their efforts, and Bakhmeteff had been warmly complimentary of Sapojnikov at his final committee meeting. Zaluboffsky's authority to remove Bakhmeteff was somewhat obscure, as Bakhmeteff was not a government employee. He was, however, stripped from his positions on the various committees, and by November 23, 1916, was no longer attending the meetings of the Anglo-Russian Sub-Committee. He returned to Russia shortly after. Bakhmeteff's removal later created complications for Zaluboffsky. Bakhmeteff would reach Russia in time to assume a post as an assistant minister of trade and industry for the Provisional Government and would later return to the United States as the ambassador—and Zaluboffsky's boss.

In October, the Ministry of Munitions proposed that General Minchin be relieved as the head of British inspection in America and henceforth focus all his efforts on the Anglo-Russian Sub-Committee and other Russian liaison duties. Minchin had accepted the appointment to the sub-committee in June as an addition to his regular duties, with the understanding that his deputy, Colonel R. L. Kenyon, would oversee the day-to-day requirements of British contracts. The ministry now sought to separate the two positions, while simultaneously promoting Minchin to major general. Despite his elevation to higher rank, Minchin was unequivocal that the proposal was a mistake for the war effort. Minchin understood that formal regulations could never effectively bind the Russians, and that his influence on Russian supply depended on his personal relations with his counterparts. While his official position gave him authority in the Anglo-Russian Sub-Committee, it alone brought him little influence over the inspections controlled by the Russian Technical

Bureau. Minchin's position in charge of British inspection gave him personal credibility with the Russians, and placed the entire British inspection effort at the disposal of his Russian liaison mission. Minchin had gained considerable influence by offering practical assistance to the Russians. "We have," he noted, "inspected metal for them, given them information ... cooperated with them and there has been a marked increase of cordiality and mutual respect as a result."[19] Despite his protests that the new arrangement would damage efforts to improve Russian inspection, Minchin was relieved of his British inspection post and Colonel Kenyon assumed his duties as head of British inspection.[20]

The first Anglo-Russian Sub-Committee meeting chaired by General Zaluboffsky appropriately enough dealt primarily with the Canadian Car contract. The company had received the sub-committee's proposal and had countered, requesting that only $2 million in penalties and interest be imposed on it and altering the proposed dates of completion. The sub-committee dictated a response, accepting the $2 million, but reiterating that 1.5 million unfilled high explosive shells had to be completed by November 15, with these shells and an additional 1 million, loaded and delivered by December 31. "We presented the proposed contracts for the purpose of giving assistance," the sub-committee wrote. "Our discussion is final and we will enter into no further discussions. Unless you consent ... we will ... proceed under existing ... contracts."[21]

A unique problem of mutual interest to the British and Russian delegations was German sabotage. While the First World War, like most conflicts, generated its own "spy mania," American neutrality provided an unusually permissive environment for German covert operations. During late 1914 and early 1915, the German embassy placed fraudulent orders for war materials with American manufacturers in an attempt to divert capacity from the Allies.[22] One German naval officer, Captain Franz von Rintelen, took the reverse approach, creating a false company that contracted with the Russians for the delivery of a wide variety of war supplies. The company either failed to deliver, or, in several cases, provided supplies sabotaged with time delayed incendiary devices to destroy the transporting ships, after which the company dissolved and disappeared.[23] While these paper ruses pointed out the disorder and vulnerability of the early supply efforts, it is doubtful that they significantly hurt the Allied supply effort.

More significant for British and Russian supply efforts, however, was the active sabotage campaign begun in early 1915.[24] An explosion at the Roebling Wire and Cable Company plant in Trenton, New Jersey on January 1, 1915, probably marked the opening of the German campaign. Before April 1917, there would be almost 200 explosions involving war supplies, factories and transportation attributed to German actions.[25] On an ongoing basis, German agents used a network of hired persons, often Irish nationalists, to infiltrate incendiary devices onboard Allied merchant shipping.[26]

The July 30, 1916 explosion at the Black Tom Port Facility, New Jersey, represented the acme of the German effort. Black Tom was a rail yard where cargoes were shifted from rail car to barge for transport to waiting merchant ships. While cargoes were not officially permitted to remain overnight, the shortage of merchant ships had resulted in a backup of tons of explosive military supplies. The resulting detonation was felt in New York City. Though the official cause of the blast was listed as carelessness, the Russian government believed otherwise and sued the company operating the terminal, charging that their lax security permitted the loss of their munitions.[27] The supply committee also attempted to recover losses from certain munitions suppliers, arguing that the shells delivered to Black Tom had not been accepted by the lighterage company which would transport them to the merchant ship. Since Black Tom was merely a holding yard, the Russians argued that the shells had never been delivered and under contract were to be replaced by the manufacturer.[28]

Six months after the Black Tom explosion, the Russians were hit again. On January 11, 1917, the Kingsland, New Jersey plant of the Canadian Car and Foundry Company, employed almost exclusively producing shells for the Russians, was destroyed in an explosion-filled four hour fire. Some half million Russian three-inch shells were lost. While the experience of Black Tom had caused the Canadian Car and Foundry Company to install a security fence and guards to the plant, these measures could not prevent sabotage by an employee. Theodore Wozniak, an ethnic Pole from the Austrian portion of Galicia, had initiated the explosion from his own work bench. Incredibly, he had gained employment at Canadian Car through the recommendation of a Russian vice consul in New York, Dmitri Florinsky. Florinsky had vouched for Wozniak once before, issuing him a permit to visit his home in Galicia.[29] Twice in the month before the explosion, Wozniak had written the artillery commission of the Russian Supply Committee warning of carelessness and unsafe practices at the plant and predicting catastrophe. The British Secret Service had been warned that Wozniak would infiltrate the Kingsland plant, but it is doubtful that this warning was passed to the Russians and Canadian Car.[30] With the loss of the Kingsland plant, built expressly for war production by British loans and advances, the question of the Canadian Car contracts became academic. There was simply no way the company could fulfill the Russian orders, and the Anglo-Russian Sub-Committee ceased discussing the matter.

During October 1916, the Russian Council of Ministers informed the Allied governments that it would ratify the resolutions of the June Paris Conference provided that Britain and France signed a separate, secret provision. The essential tenet of the proposed agreement was that, while each government agreed to follow the results of the June conference, they would be free to disregard them if they were not in their own national interest. Here in open forum was the critical problem with Russian participation in the coalition—the Russian government at the highest levels declined to compromise its national interest in support of its Allies.[31]

An Inter-Allied Supply Conference was held in London on November 8–10, 1916. The primary task of the attendees was to determine what munitions would be required to support the coming year of military operations. As had become their wont, the Russian delegation, again headed by Colonel Beliaev, placed extravagant demands before the committee. The issue of heavy artillery had never been settled after the July conference, and Beliaev requested almost 1,100 heavy pieces, a figure representing most of the Allies' annual production. Lloyd George expressed his skepticism of the British ability to fill the request, but did not entirely dismiss it. Thomas, weighing in for France, essentially put the Russians on notice that France also expected a part of the annual British artillery production. There were, he emphasized, other considerations beyond simple numbers. Could the Russians secure ammunition for so many pieces? Could they conceivably ship them to Russia, much less the front? The British, set up as arbiters between two Allies, deferred decision. Shortly after the conference, the British would authorize a generous transfer of artillery to the Russians, though still slightly less than half what had been requested.[32]

While the issue of artillery shells remained, the Russians tried a new approach to secure the railroad supplies they felt so critical. On November 17, 1916, the Russian minister of commerce informed the British ambassador that the long-awaited Murman rail line would be ready for operation in early 1917. With the announcement, Trepov also requested British permission to resume independent orders of rail supplies from the United States. The Foreign Office believed it politically expedient to grant permission, but the Treasury and the Ministry of Munitions were absolutely opposed. The Ministry of Munitions pointed out the "the total requirement of the Allies both for railway material and for steel products generally are substantially in excess of the [capacity of the] American market," and that thus Russian orders would only be at the expense of competing Allied requirements.[33]

While the issue of artillery continued to be debated, the Russian government's small arms orders were in serious difficulty. Despite ongoing inspection problems, Westinghouse, the largest Russian rifle contractor, had ultimately reached a production rate of 3,500 rifles per day. While it was largely satisfying the terms of its original contract, it was sustaining tremendous ongoing financial losses. By January 1917, the losses were too great to sustain, and the company refused to continue production until the British government protected it from further losses. Several months of negotiations ensued between Westinghouse and the British government, with the Russians as an outside party. In order to avoid the complete bankruptcy of a major weapons supplier, the British government finally signed a supplemental contract on May 1, 1917. In it, the parties agreed to reduce the total number of rifles to be delivered to 1 million, to increase the price per rifle by six dollars, to indemnify the company from any loss of more than $5 million in the completion of the contract and, most importantly, to pay the company $1.5 million per month regardless of the number of rifles delivered during the month. The figure of 1 million rifles was considered that lowest figure that would exhaust the considerable raw materials and parts already on hand. The supplemental contract also gave the British government three options to order as many as 800,000 additional rifles. Finally, once the production of the requested rifles was concluded, all assets Westinghouse had acquired to manufacture rifles would be liquidated and the proceeds divided between Westinghouse and the British government.[34]

5

The Zemsky Buy a Railroad: A Case Study

The involvement of non-governmental organizations in traditionally government functions, with or without governmental approval, gave rise to a series of difficult interactions between American industry and Russian civil society. Examining one specific order as a case study forces issues usually presented as generalizations into high relief and permits a better view of the problems that arose with Tsarist Russians and American capitalists working together. This study examines the series of orders placed with the American Locomotive Company in 1916 and 1917 by zemstvo representatives in the United States.

The selection of a railway supply order reflects the critical nature of these materials for the Russian war effort. Like so many of the mechanisms of modern industry in the empire, the Russian rail system at the beginning of the First World War was the product of considerable labor and sacrifice on the part of the government and population—and was inadequate for the task at hand. The increasingly mobile nature of warfare in the Industrial Age and the distances inherent in the vast Russian expanses made the empire particularly dependent on a capable rail system. Once mobilized, the average soldier of German or Austro-Hungarian armies had to be transported less than two hundred miles, whereas Russian troops averaged five hundred.[1] Yet the Russian Empire entered the war with the least capable rail network in Europe by every measure, as well as a serious shortage of rolling stock of all descriptions for what railroads it did possess.[2] These transport limitations made themselves felt in both military and civilian supply and directly in military operations. General Brusilov, for example, chose not to rely on distant reinforcements during his 1916 offensive, commenting that given the Russian railway system, "I knew that while we were entraining and transporting one army corps, the Germans would manage to transport three or four."[3] Railway improvements were a high wartime priority, and testimony before the State Duma in March 1916 noted that some 52,000 railcars and 900 locomotives were pending delivery.[4]

If the lack of transportation infrastructure was damaging in European Russia, it was absolutely crippling in the Caucasus. Diplomatic and political maneuvering between the Great Powers over Turkish belligerence had delayed the onset of war in the region, but in late October 1914, the Turkish Fleet, under the command of a German rear-admiral, forced the issue by attacking the Russian Black Sea coast. The Russian declaration of war followed four days later.[5] Thrust into war, the Turkish Army hastened to attack Russian forces in the Caucasus. Already beginning to face supply and transportation problems on the main front, the Russians viewed the opening of an additional front with alarm and requested assistance from the Allies.[6] Fortunately, in the Turkish Army the Russians had a foe more poorly supplied and led than themselves, and by January 1915 the initial offensive had been defeated with the Turkish forces sustaining 86 percent losses.[7] Throughout the war, military operations in the Caucasus were characterized by extended supply lines over difficult terrain. Given over to offensive action, Russian forces in the region faced the unenviable prospect of creating their lines of communication as they advanced.

This lack of infrastructure gave the work of the zemstvos in the Caucasus what the union's official report called its "special character." The Caucasus Front opened after extensive experience in the Western areas had made the Zemgor an integral part of the army establishment. Generally, the practical necessities of war insured the Zemgor was well received by military commanders even as the government regarded the organization with increasing suspicion. Shortly after the opening of the front, the chief of the Sanitation and Evacuation Department, Prince Alexander Oldenburg, requested the Zemgor accept exclusive responsibility for the handling of casualties in the Caucasus.[8] The union took pains to emphasize that the resulting plan and the government funding that made it possible were "sanctioned by His Majesty's Viceroy of the Caucasus." It is little wonder that the union chose to emphasize what government approval the Zemgor could claim. Prince Lvov, president of the Union of Zemstvos and later president of the Provisional Government, wrote that the union existed to do "things which the government was unable to do."[9] The history of the zemstvo movement in the war is a recurring tale of the voluntary organization moving to satisfy quasi-governmental functions with limited governmental approval. Even partisans of the voluntary organizations granted that they were prone to interpret their charter in the broadest possible terms.[10]

In the case of the Caucasus, the army request to handle casualties resulted in the Zemgor taking responsibility for an extensive transportation network, ostensibly as part of its charter to facilitate medical evacuation. By January 1916, in addition to the 30,000 hospital beds it provided, the union undertook the maintenance of the roads to Batum, Kars, Olta and Igdir, each of which was also a significant supply route to the forward areas. Conditions on the latter three roads required the deployment of a specialized zemstvo medical and feeding detachment that managed a network of pack animals and motor cars staged along the roadway. Casualties were transported through the tenable sections of the road by car, then dismounted to cross higher altitude areas by sled or pack animal until reaching the next station where motor transport was staged.[11]

That the union's attention would include the railroads in the Caucasus can hardly be considered surprising. In addition to its interest in transport, the union had increasingly moved through 1915 to supply military needs by acting directly as a broker between industry and individual military units, completely bypassing the military supply system. Further, the union had experience in railroad supply and operation because of the extensive network of hospital trains it purchased and operated on the Western Front.[12] The immediate impetus for the overseas locomotive order was the Russian military advance. The Russian offensive in January 1916, launched to preempt an offensive by Turkish forces freed by the Allied withdrawal from Gallipoli, enjoyed considerable success. By mid–February, an advance of over fifty miles on a seventy-mile front had yielded the city of Erzerum, captured 327 Turkish guns and further extended the Russian rail supply lines.[13] When faced with this new requirement, the Russian forces in the Caucasus expressed a need for seventy railroad engines and 670 pieces of rolling stock suitable for the rail lines running to their forward supply centers. The request was passed directly to the Zemgor.[14]

Once the request reached the Zemgor, a number of factors probably entered into the decision to send this particular locomotive order to a foreign supplier. By May 1916 according to the Russian minister of foreign affairs, Russia had placed about $1 billion in orders in the United States, and both the Russian government and the union were intimately familiar with the process for ordering equipment from abroad.[15] Ordering from abroad bypassed much of the Russian bureaucracy and the problems of finding and dealing with Russian suppliers. Ordering abroad also introduced the possibility that British credits could be used for the purchase. Indeed, in the case of the Caucasus locomotives, the British government, "with the cooperation of the late Lord Kitchener, appropriated in the middle of March 1916, $1,370,000 for the purchase" of the required locomotives and rolling stock, as well as "spare parts for the same, a few lathes for the repair works, and also for the payment of the shipping expenses." [16] Not only did Kitchener have a long-term interest in the Russian Front, but the successful Russian operation against Ezerum over difficult terrain impressed many Allied observers.[17]

For heavy equipment, given the commitment of British and French manufacturers to munitions, an order abroad meant an order in America. By March 1916, testimony in the State Duma indicated that over 13,000 rail cars had been ordered from American suppliers.[18] Even prior to the war, American manufacturers were no strangers to the Russian railroad market. Through the 1890s, Baldwin Locomotive sold 500 locomotives to the Trans-Siberian Railroad, as well as over 200 to various roads in European Russia, and maintained a permanent agent in Saint Petersburg.[19] This trade had been severely restricted beginning in 1902 when the Ministry of Ways and Communications introduced a committee to approve overseas orders for locomotives and rolling stock, effectively stifling the trade. [20]

The wartime lifting of these restrictions naturally attracted major American manufacturers back to the Russian market. The largest was the American Locomotive Company, which had been formed in 1901 by the merger of ten separate locomotive manufacturers. In 1917, it was ranked by *Forbes* as the 61st largest company in the United States, and, together with the Baldwin Locomotive Works and the Lima Locomotive Works, represented virtually all American locomotive construction at the turn of the century.[21] Technically, the company appeared well suited for the task of supplying locomotives to the Russian military. Like many American concerns doing business with the Russians, however, they were to find that the gulf of experience and expectations between American capitalists and Russian functionaries would produce a series of orders unique in their complications.

Sensing that the war offered a means to re-enter the once lucrative Russian market, American Locomotive had moved quickly to offer its services. On October 7, 1914, the secretary of the American Manufacturers Export Association wrote the commercial attaché of the Russian embassy, Constantine Medzikhovsky, seeking "a letter of introduction ... to the secretary of commerce in Russia" on behalf of Charles M. Muchnic, manager of the Foreign Department of the American Locomotive Company and an officer of the export association. Muchnic, the letter explained, was "contemplating a trip in the near future to various European cities, including possibly Petrograd, in the interests of his concern."[22] Muchnic would later become a key figure in the union's orders with American Locomotive. By the time of the zemstvo order, the firm also had some experience with Russian munitions contracts, serving as a major subcontractor on the Canadian Car shell order. The firm had proved canny enough to purchase $500,000 worth of specialized munitions production equipment in early 1915, before contracts were finalized, assessing that, if the orders fell through, the munitions market would insure a profit on the resale of the equipment.[23]

The representatives of the Zemstvo Union in the United States, created for just such a purpose, were the logical personnel to negotiate and conclude the order, and they commenced work.[24] They were, however, very nearly pre-empted by their counterparts at home. The international representatives of American manufacturers posed a continuing problem throughout the war. Naturally, these salesmen were anxious to conclude their part of the lucrative war trade. The prospect of parallel negotiations with the same supplier, as well as the manifold issues of coordination led most Allies to place orders only through a single commission and rely on the local manufacturers' representatives only as product experts. Within each government, however, trade representatives could find agencies that were exempt or would bypass the official channels. If this phenomenon was problematic in Britain, it was more so in the less-centralized Russian effort. On approaching the American Locomotive Company in mid–April, the union office in New York was informed that "on March 23rd we [American Locomotive] received a cablegram from our representative in Petrograd ... advising that a contract had been awarded to us by the Zemstvo-Souiz [*sic*] for the War Department, subject only to confirmation by the London Finance Bureau." The offering price was $4,965.00 per engine, plus an additional $350.00 to cover optional equipment that would permit the locomotives to burn oil as well as coal. As the union was clearly interested in quick delivery, the firm advised that the first engine could be finished within 60 days from the confirmation of the order, with all 70 engines done within 110 days.[25] The union representative spent much of the remainder of the month determining exactly what offers had been made to whom. In the meantime, the union had requested that American Locomotive hold their offer open for three weeks. Citing "the extraordinary conditions of the steel market," the firm declined, noting that "the prices we gave you were subject to acceptance during last month, and ... you must impress upon your committee in London and Moscow the advisability of acting more promptly."[26]

American Locomotive finally accepted the order, which it designated #C-467. Once formalized, the Russian committee was obliged to provide American Locomotive with inspectors for the soon-to-be-completed engines. The first and primary Russian inspector, Professor Michel Gololoboff, arrived in Paterson, New Jersey, in July and installed himself at Kelsey House near the factory.[27] He was soon joined by at least three other Zemgor representatives. Inspection was one of the most consistent causes of complaint for American manufacturers of Russian orders, and the American Locomotive order was to prove no exception. Where Russian inspectors were apt to see deviations from the contract, American manufacturers saw deviations to the contract. Exactly a month after Gololoboff's arrival at the works, Muchnic felt compelled to inform him that "the numerous changes that have been made since your arrival here ... necessitated discarding of materials ordered and the ordering of new materials." As a result, the shipment of the seventy engines would "naturally be delayed."[28] When the Pekosnarm demanded an explanation for the delay, Gololoboff conceded that the delay was "caused partly by our indications to [American Locomotive] not to alter specifications." But, he argued that the Russian inspectors had "required nothing above specifications" but "in contrary have accepted alterations" to facilitate the order.[29] It is certainly possible that American Locomotive underestimated the effect of the considerable custom work the Russians typically demanded on their foreign-produced locomotives. However, the pattern of Russian inspections during the war suggests that unfamiliarity with American manufacturing practices caused unnecessary delays.

Whatever the cause, the prospect of delay raised concern both in America and Russia. Muchnic had noted that the order could still be completed in "ample time for shipment to Archangel before the port is closed for the winter," but given the difficulties in transport any delay was problematic.[30] Delaying the order disrupted the production schedule for the entire Paterson plant, delaying other war orders. The next major order due had been placed by the British government and was intended for the Egyptian State Railway. On August 25, 1916, the export department at J. P. Morgan, acting in the name of General Minchin as well as Morgan, cabled the Ministry of Munitions informing them of the delay in the Russian order. The Russians had requested that work on the Egyptian order be delayed for one month to facilitate their shipment via Arkhangel'sk prior to its winter closure. Noting the "difficulties of transport of locomotives via Siberia and the urgent necessity for these locomotives for Caucasus operations," Morgan recommended accepting the delay of the Egyptian order.[31] The same day, Professor Astroff, the senior representative of the Zemstvo in America, also telegraphed General Hermonious to inform the London Committee of the problem.[32] In early September, the British government replied via Morgan that the Egyptian order could be delayed.[33]

The delays in production both highlighted and exacerbated the seemingly simple problem of arranging transportation for the completed locomotives. By fall 1916, the increasing tide of Allied war orders, compounded by typical heavy seasonal demand, had resulted in the number of freight car loads requiring shipment exceeding the amount of available rolling stock by 114,908 car loads.[34] While a locomotive manufacturer was probably in a position to circumvent this difficulty, the more acute problem of ocean transport dogged the union. While the contract clearly called for American Locomotive to deliver "free alongside" (FAS) a steamer provided by the union, the practical issue of who among the Russians was arranging transportation seemed to have evaded both the Russian delegation and American Locomotive. Initially, American Locomotive was under the impression that the redoubtable Medzikhovsky had responsibility for shipping. He quickly clarified that while he, as the commercial attaché, had conveyed the Russian government's official permission for the locomotives to be admitted to Arkhangel'sk "this ... did not mean that I was to ship them as I have no instructions ... and no information about this order." Rather, he recommended that American Locomotive contact either the union office in New York or the Russian inspector currently working at the American factory.[35] Muchnic chose the closest representative, Professor Gololoboff, and informed him that "doubtless you and your committee will arrange for the transportation of these locomotives."[36] It was a statement based more on hope than fact.

As locomotives began to be completed in August, the Russian delegation had still not arranged transportation for them. Unable to deliver alongside a steamer and thus satisfy the contract requirement for deck papers, American Locomotive requested to be paid based on units completed and stored at the Paterson plant. By the end of August, some fifteen engines were waiting shipment there with two more being completed each day.[37] The committee managed to reduce the backlog in September, when Gololoboff reported that twenty-eight of the thirty units completed had been shipped on board the Russian Volunteer Fleet freighter *Turgat*. The freighter *Omsk* was scheduled to ship another thirty in the near future.

Wartime shipping schedules, however, were to prove unreliable, particularly when dealing with the Russian Volunteer Fleet. In mid–October the manager at the Paterson plant addressed a letter to Muchnic, appealing for his help in moving the remaining Russian engines. Twenty-two of them remained at the factory, creating a "very congested condition" and complicating the completion of the delayed Egyptian order. From the manager's comments it is clear that the transport aboard the *Omsk* did not occur, as the locomotives shipped to the New York piers other than those shipped on *Turgat* remained.[38] The locomotives that the committee and the war effort so urgently required were going nowhere. Addressing the problem to the Russian Committee, Muchnic noted that, aside from the inconvenience, leaving the engines at the factory:

> is having a demoralizing effect upon our men who have been urged to complete the locomotives with the utmost despatch [sic] possible. We cannot call upon our men to exert their best efforts, to work overtime if necessary, in order to complete locomotives within contract time and when such locomotives are completed to have them stored in our yards for days and weeks without being shipped.[39]

The situation was serious enough that Professor Astroff had departed for Britain three days prior to discuss Russian shipping needs. The delegation summed it up succinctly in their October 24 telegram to Petrograd—"cannot ship rest no steamers."[40] The last engines of order C-467 would remain in the United States, sitting at the Russian Volunteer Fleet pier in New York, until at least early the next year, and probably remained until the commission's liquidation.

The committee's efforts to solve the transportation problem were no doubt complicated by the personal disagreements that had developed among the zemstvo representatives in Paterson. Gololoboff clearly fancied himself first among the delegation. By early September, the situation had caused four remaining officials, but particularly Inspector Meyer, to complain to Petrograd. In response, the Pekosnarm informed Gololoboff that the Petrograd Committee had given his four colleagues "equal rights with collegial decision of matters."[41] Since this arrangement was not working, the Petrograd Committee authorized Professor Astroff "to arrange henceforth in Pekosnarm's name mutual relations between members of commission and altar [*sic*] instructions personally."[42] The new relationship was obviously unsatisfactory. Within four days, five inspectors signed a telegram to the Petrograd Committee asserting that Gololoboff was obstructing the work of the committee with "his incapacity to organize, allowance to works and with reaction in all questions." To this point, his colleagues claimed that they had "tried all measures to repair situation include [*sic*] explanation [to Professor] Astroff ... together labor is impossible."[43] The next day Petrograd replied: Gololoboff, whose planned assignment in America had almost expired, was to return to Russia as planned; Meyer, who had sought an extension in the United States, had been denied and was to return to Russia as well. A month later, Inspector Vasilieff noted in a telegram to Petrograd that Meyer and Gololoboff had both departed for home on September 30—Meyer via Arkhangel'sk and Gololoboff via Vladivostok.[44]

Even as collegial relations were being restored among the Russian delegation, a new problem arose as the Russians attempted to secure spare parts that had been authorized as part of the initial locomotive purchase. When on October 1, 1916, the Zemstvo representatives offered their list of spare parts to be added to the locomotive shipment, they expected a price quote that reflected cost plus ten percent. The response from American Locomotive was, in their view, entirely too expensive, and the union requested "in view of the high quotations on the spare parts for our locomotives ... a list of relative prices on those parts, accompanying same by detailed documents which prove the cost of fabrication."[45] Muchnic replied that the purchase of spare parts on a cost basis applied only to parts ordered with the locomotives and produced at the same time. The union had not executed this option in April "although we ... continually warned you that the prices of materials and labor are constantly rising."[46] In fall 1916, prices in America had increased almost 180% since June 1914, and based on the added cost resulting from the delay in the initial locomotive order it ought to have been evident to the union that delay in placing any order in such an economy would add considerably to its cost.[47] Despite this observation, union representatives began what was to be a torturous four-month negotiation over the particulars of the spare parts contract. The union wanted to pay following delivery on board the steamer rather than to the pier. Mindful of the continued transport difficulties with the locomotive order, American Locomotive declined, observing that "there is uncertainty as to whether you will have steamers ready." The union sought to stipulate the thickness and finish of the wooden shipping boxes, as well as the finish of all the parts. The union sought to eliminate all risk or uncertainty from the order, and so doing failed to account for the uncertainty of the war.[48]

By January, the usually diplomatic Muchnic was clearly becoming exasperated with the negotiations. He explained that:

> Due to the abnormal conditions existing at the present time, we regret that we cannot accept an order from you except on the conditions as stipulated by our attorneys. Most of our transactions running into very large sums of money are covered by contracts that are very brief and simple and are largely based on good faith between the two contracting parties. The wording to which you take exception in our contract is largely brought about by your not accepting our formal proposition covering the execution of the order for your spareparts [sic] and which was worded the same as hundreds of similar propositions that we make almost daily and which no one ever questions. You submitted to us a contract which was made to tie us down absolutely to every detail and which we naturally had to submit to our attorneys ... considerable time has been lost....[49]

As a result, Muchnic explained, the prices at which the spare parts had been offered had expired, and it would be necessary for American Locomotive to adjust the order. On February 13, 1917, the order for $24,780.93 in spare parts was finally closed, delivery to be made no later than June 3, 1917.[50]

Even as the spare parts issue was drawing to a close, the Pekosnarm plunged further into the American market. During the spring, the Caucasus Army had received the first of the initial American Locomotives and had pronounced them fit for service. On this basis, it had requested an additional order be placed and in early April Vasilieff found himself requesting Muchnic provide the cost and delivery time for an additional sixty to seventy locomotives.[51] The resulting quote came as a shock to the Russians, who had failed to account for the effects of wartime inflation. The American entry into the war in mid–April further complicated the negotiation. Placing an order for a military commodity such as railroad engines suddenly required the approval of the Council of National Defense, which was moving to coordinate American industrial efforts.[52] The Russians met at least twice with the chairman of the council, Bernard Baruch, who consented to place the order. The Russians explained that the estimates of both American Locomotive and Baldwin were running between $10,500 and $11,000, a 90 percent increase over the year. While smaller manufacturers could offer better terms, only the major manufacturers could deliver before the winter closure of Arkhangel'sk. The appeal for government intervention provided no help.[53] When order #C-517 was finally signed with American Locomotive in July, the committee agreed to purchase 68 locomotives at $12,560 each. Learning from the previous transportation problems, American Locomotive insisted that the completed locomotives be accepted at the plant, and that the Russians provide rail transport from the plant within five days of their final inspection. If the Russians failed, they would be charged for the storage of the engines.[54]

This forethought, however, was to no avail. The already poor state of rail traffic in the United States worsened as industry moved to war production, and the delivery of certain minor parts for the engines was delayed. By February, these missing parts were cited by the Russians as they refused delivery of the locomotives, despite 22 of them having been tested and ten already boxed for shipping. An exasperated Muchnic wrote the committee that American Locomotive "did not expect your present attitude but rather anticipated that you would trust our Company" and that American required the payments due on acceptance "to carry out our important contracts for this government and the Allies."[55] Between the lines, however, is the fact that by not signing for the locomotives, the Russians were not required to move them; and all 68 engines in the order would remain at Paterson well after completion.

Even as the second order was in negotiation, the initial order C-467 for the original seventy locomotives, completed over a year ago, remained an issue for American Locomotive. The terms of the contract called for a representative of the company to assist in the set-up and operation of the locomotives during a one-year warranty period. The delays in initial delivery and transport to Russia, while considerable, were minor compared to the delay involved in assembling the locomotives on Russian soil. By August 1917, only 23 engines had been set up. At this rate, the set-up process threatened to take more than a year, and the American engineers involved were "urgently needed ... in connection with other contracts."[56] Beyond the expense of maintaining personnel in Russia, the delay in set-up threatened to hold almost indefinitely the financial settlement of the contract. The final 3 percent of the contract was payable after the conclusion of the warranty period, which itself could not begin until the engines were in operation. American Locomotive had predicated the contract on "the assumption, based on many years of experience, that the assembling of the 70 engines would consume at the outside two months." Given the delays, in October, American requested full payment for the order.[57]

Not until June 1918, did the final financial settlement of both locomotive contracts take place. The Pekosnarm sent Muchnic a check for $35.00, and indicated that as the Pekosnarm would be "suspending" American operations in the near future, correspondence should be addressed to the Supply Division of the Russian embassy.[58]

By April 1918, events had made the 68 completed locomotives stored at Paterson superfluous. Two revolutions after the initial order, the Caucasus Army and its transportation requirements had ceased to exist. The commission requested that American Locomotive assist in selling the engines, a request the company quickly passed to the Council of National Defense. The council first addressed the question to the respective Allied purchasing agents in the United States, then to the United States Railroad Administration. By August, each agency, as well as the War Department, had refused to purchase the Russian engines.[59]

While the exact fate of the 68 Russian locomotives after September cannot be determined, it is doubtful that a nation at war and short of locomotives would ignore a possible source of transport. In December 1917, the United States government had taken control of all railroads under the United States Railroad Administration (USRA). Faced with its own problem of securing locomotives for growing wartime demand, the USRA mandated a series of standardized designs, with all purchasing being negotiated and finalized through a USRA Purchasing Committee.[60] As an emergency measure, it also purchased approximately 200 of the 2-10-0 ("Decapod") locomotives produced by American Locomotive and Baldwin under Russian government contract.[61] While reportedly disparaged for their European appearance, the Russian 2-10-0s generally performed well on American rails. Adapting these locomotives to American use posed the same challenges which would have affected the Caucasus engines, and there is no reason to believe the smaller 0-6-0s from the zemstvo contract could not have been used.[62]

The locomotives that had been delivered to the Caucasus became prizes in the disintegration of the Russian Empire. The territory containing most of the engines was part of that returned to Turkey under the terms of the Treaty of Brest-Litovsk.[63] Cut off from most news themselves, the Russians wrote one of the former Paterson plant managers in September 1918, "to express to you our greatest appreciation and thanks" and to let him know what had become of the locomotives he had helped build:

> The only information we have had stated that 42 of them were assembled ... but Mr. Robert Brown, who recently came from Russia, informed us that 27 of our locomotives ... were taken by Turks. What happened to the others nobody can say.[64]

6

The Liberals in Control

The installation of the Provisional Government in February 1917 represented the political ascendance of Russian liberalism. Prince Lvov, head of the Union of Zemstvos, became president, while Paul Miliukov assumed duties as foreign minister. Passionately committed to the continuation of the war, the Provisional Government eagerly sought to continue and expand foreign supply of Russian forces. Had the stifling effect of the Tsarist government been the key reason for the astonishing inefficiency of Russian purchasing in the United States, the months of Provisional Government rule should have represented the most productive months of the Allied supply relationship. Instead, the Provisional Government continued many of the same errors of the previous regime, proving that it, too, was ill equipped to handle such issues.

Once the pro-war views of the new government had been established within Allied circles, the earnest hope was that a Russian democracy would represent a more stable, reliable and honorable partner.[1] The most widespread, if not particularly well informed, view in official circles was that the Russian people supported the war, even if they did not support their government. The Provisional Government, led by a coterie of western oriented liberals largely known in Allied capitals, tried to feed this idea and probably sincerely believed it. Prince Lvov had informed a visiting French delegation in February 1917 that:

> Russia is filled with belief in the successful ending of the war, but she clearly recognizes that the principal danger of the present position is not from without but from within the country and that ... government supported by representatives of the people and capable of containing the whole vital forces of the nation are the ... absolutely essential conditions for the attainment of victory.[2]

Here the "ministry of public confidence" that Russian liberals had been calling for since late 1915 was being presented as an aid to the Allied effort.

Certainly that was the official verdict of the Russian Supply Commission in America. The commission had received its first official notice of the events in Petrograd on March 15, 1917, two days after the Duma Committee formed a Provisional Government. The true shock arrived on March 21, when a cablegram addressed to the military agent in the United States arrived from Petrograd:

> In addition to the radio-telegram transmitted on the 3rd of March [o.s.] on this subject, I report that on March 2 [o.s.], the Emperor abdicated for himself and his son in favor of the Grand Duke Michael Alexandrovich. The latest in the transformation is that he will only take supreme power if such is the will of the people, expressed by a Constituent Assembly. All the major directorates of the War Ministry continue without exception to function under the authority of the Provisional Government. Life gradually settles into its own framework, and quite successfully. The title of "lower ranks" is replaced by the term "soldiers." Soldiers are required to refer to superiors politely, but superiors are addressed personally. For example, 'Citizen General or Colonel and so on.'[3]

Shortly after this message, the Pekosnarm representatives received a cable from their superiors assuring them that the:

> new Provisional Government [is] trusted by population [and] goes on working for needs of the Army. Committee asks Commission to use utmost efforts if fulfilling intrusted [sic] work for benefit [of] our country.[4]

The committee replied that "trusting in the great future of Russia, we use every effort in work for army needs and benefit our country."[5]

The prospects for the Russian Commission in America were buoyed when the United States became the first nation to recognize the Provisional

Government. The decision to recognize the shift in power had actually been made by Washington on March 20, before the Russian Commission in New York had officially been apprised of the situation. Paul Miliukov, installed as the foreign minister, received Ambassador Francis on the morning of March 22.[6]

The ascendance of liberal elements within Russian supply efforts was insured by the Provisional Government's diplomatic legation to America. When the Provisional Government sent its first formal representatives to the United States in April 1917, Professor Boris A. Bakhmeteff, the former Central War-Industries Committee representative to the Russian Supply Commission, chaired the delegation. Named initially as the Provisional Government's assistant minister of trade and industry, Bakhmeteff was selected to head the new government's "Extraordinary Embassy" to the United States and then remain as the permanent ambassador of the Provisional Government. Accompanied by an entourage of about forty other officials representing the Ministries of War, Agriculture, Finance and Ways and Communications, Bakhmeteff traveled across Siberia to Japan, and across the United States to Washington, D.C., in what came to resemble a triumphal procession. Arriving in Washington, Bakhmeteff was invited to address both the House of Representatives and the Senate, was officially received by President Wilson and laid a wreath at Washington's tomb at Mount Vernon. William Jennings Bryan, the secretary of war, the army chief of staff, and the head of the American Red Cross all called on the mission. At each venue, Bakhmeteff spread his message that Russia and the United States were now "sister democracies" and that Russia was worthy of wholehearted American support.[7]

In New York, the Russian community, official and unofficial, turned out to greet the new ambassador. The *New York Times* described the welcome at City Hall where "thousands of men and women ... born in Russia under the Old Regime who had been forced to flee from persecution religious or political ... acclaimed the representative of the new free Government of their native land."[8] Significantly, Professor Sakhnovsky, the senior zemstvo representative in America, and not a government official, led the official festivities.[9]

The shift in governments caused new attention in the American press to the various representatives of Russian civil society in the war effort. This may be in part due to increased public awareness of Russian liberalism and in part a greater willingness of non-governmental representatives to speak out, confident that they were no longer marked for government stigma. In June, the senior representatives in New York of the War Industries Committee and the Union of Zemstvos and Towns signed a joint letter to the *New York Times* defending the role of socialists in the new government:

> The word "Socialist" still arouses in a portion of the American public the idea of a man ... setting aflame everything in his path. They seem to forget that ... in the British, French and Italian Cabinets, Socialists are among the most prominent members.[10]

In August, the *New York Times* magazine did an extended and complimentary profile of Alexander Sakhnovsky, representative of the Union of Towns and Cities in the U.S., citing him as "a splendid example ... for the men of every nation."[11]

As ambassador, Bakhmeteff assumed control of all Russian purchasing efforts in the United States. Bakhmeteff was accompanied from Russia by Colonel Oranovski, vice president of the Munitions Committee in New York. Upon reaching the Pacific Coast of the United States, Bakhmeteff requested that General Khrabroff, chief of the artillery commission, meet him on his arrival in Washington.[12] General Zaluboffsky, who had evicted Bakhmeteff from the Supply Commission in August of the previous year, was himself relieved and ordered to return to Russia, while General Khrabroff assumed leadership of the Supply Commission.[13]

One of the most notable members of the Bakhmeteff delegation was Professor Lomonosov. Listed in American documents as a representative of the "Railway Office," Lomonosov was actually a distinguished engineer and senior railway official of the Ministry of Ways and Communications. His inclusion in the mission reflected the high priority that the new government continued to place on acquiring American railroad equipment. On his arrival in New York, he assumed leadership of the Ministry of Ways and Communications delegation within the Russian Supply Commission. During the 1905 Revolution, he had also been an active supporter of terrorist elements in the Social Democratic Party and later had played a role in obstructing the rail movement of counter-revolutionary troops during the February Revolution. His radical sympathies would return to plague Bakhmeteff.[14]

The arrival of the delegation as America was finally entering the war offered the immediate prospect of exploiting American finance and industry as a co-belligerent. The Americans had actually raised the question of American finance of Russian purchasing prior to the declaration of war on Germany. On April 3, Ambassador Francis was charged with finding "if financial aid or credit is desired by the Russian Government." If so,

Secretary Lansing authorized him to "discuss tentatively the idea that the United States Government might extend such credit." The department wanted to determine if the credit offered "would be used for the purchase of supplies in the United States, and what amount of credit would likely by required over a period of six months."[15]

The Russians responded with obvious enthusiasm. Bark informed Ambassador Francis that "Russia would expend entire proceeds in the United States by direct purchases and not through British intervention as heretofore." Presented the prospect of a new source of funding, the immediate Russian response was to use it to avoid the hated British control system. Russian needs, Bark indicated, would demand a $500 million loan "provided tonnage therefore can be secured." The prospects were small of securing shipping for an additional half billion dollars in supplies, much less their transport into the Russian interior. Russia, however, would not be denied. The American loan, Bark continued, would have to be on the same terms as previous Allied loans as it "would be injurious to the new government and humiliating to Russia if she were not granted the same terms."[16] Discussing Russia's current debts, Bark brought up the reduction in British support from the 8 million tons promised in February to 4.2 million tons. Britain, Bark explained, had also promised "$360,000,000 to pay for purchases in America during 1917 ... made by Russian commission in America but approved by England." The Russians wanted to "hold England to furnishing $360,000,000 mentioned above in addition to what we advance Russia."[17]

With Bark arranging a new source of financing, the natural instinct in the Russian bureaucracy was to secure as much of the funds as possible by quickly obligating the money. With characteristic impatience, the Russian minister of Ways and Communication telegraphed his agent in America, instructing him to:

> Immediately order to commence work 500 locomotives and 10,000 twenty-ton cars for quickest delivery. Consult American War Department. Credit terms arranged later but money considered quite sure.[18]

Faced with these instructions, Secretary Lansing informed Francis that such orders should await Russian consultation with the Treasury Department. Further, the Russians needed to understand that purchase in the United States would have to be made through an American commission empowered to place Allied orders.[19]

Unlike the British government, the United States was in a position to enforce its demand that purchasing be logically organized. The zemstvo representatives probably had the first Russian experience with the fledgling organs of American control when they placed their second locomotive order with the American Locomotive Company. On August 24, 1917, the Russian ambassador signed a memorandum between the Russian government and the secretary of the treasury, effectively consolidating in American hands Russian military orders. Three Americans, among them Bernard Baruch of the War Industries Board, were designated "a Commission through whom or with whose approval or consent all purchases in the United States of materials and supplies by ... the Government of Russia shall be made." The commission would receive Russian requirements and attempt to determine available suppliers, prices and terms, and would pass this information to the Russian Supply Commission. The memorandum was calculated both to preserve the current system of cooperation in Allied supply planning and to avoid forcing the United States to arbitrate supply decisions. "Since other foreign governments engaged in war with the enemies of the United States may have entered into similar arrangements," the memorandum stated, "it is understood that all such foreign governments shall agree among themselves as to their several requirements and as to the priorities of delivery." The Russians were

> under no obligation to make purchases of materials ... at the prices and upon the terms so submitted by the Commission, but it is agreed that [the Russian government] shall not ... make purchases in the United States otherwise than through ... the Commission.

Through the memorandum, the American achieved the control over Russian purchasing which the British government had sought for three years and failed to achieve. By fall 1917, the Americans controlled both sides of the supply equation. Through the War Industries Board, the United States government could stymie war orders it felt were disruptive. It also increasingly controlled Russian funding. Though the memorandum stipulated that nothing it contained would "impose any obligation or liability upon the United States ... to advance moneys [or] to establish credits," the United States was in the process of replacing Britain as Russia's main financier.[20]

The American entry into the war set off a furious debate over who was to finance the Russian Supply Commission and how the money was to be spent. From the British perspective, the Americans were maddeningly fair about their support of each ally, failing to appreciate the financial strain which Britain had borne for the cause. The August 24 agreement between Russia and the United States was virtually a verbatim copy of an agreement signed by Britain and the United States the same day.[21]

For their part, the British now found themselves in the role that the Russian had been playing for the past several years: a belligerent power, dependent on foreign credit, obligated to place orders through a foreign control board. The results, while better than those of the Russians, were not exemplary. In a November 1917 report, the British Purchasing Mission in the United States observed that British ministries were causing great difficulties because of their tendency to purchase through American representatives in Britain rather than through the official control board. Truly, the wheel had come full circle.[22]

Russia had initially wanted American credits to be completely independent of British funds. As British funds were already pledged for existing orders, the American money, free from British controls, could be used for new purchases. The British, however, were not amiable to Russian plans. As early as April 28, 1917, the British government began withdrawing credit from orders in the process of being placed. The *Glavnoe Artilleriiskoe Upravlenie* representatives in New York had closed a deal with the Poole Engineering Company for 80 McLean guns and 400,000 rounds of ammunition, approved through the Anglo-Russian Sub-Committee in the typical manner, only to be informed after the fact that Britain would not finance the order. At the May 3, 1917, meeting of the sub-committee, the members unanimously approved a letter to the British minister of munitions, emphasizing that the agreement of July 31, 1916, had been observed in this order and that the agreement prohibited the withdrawal of approved credit except by mutual consent. General Khrabroff, writing for the sub-committee, said that

> the decision from the British Government will highly discredit not only my position in America, but also of the Anglo-Russian Sub-Committee, that this particular case is not the only one of its kind that has happened, I am asking you to take action against the creation of such situation, which in the end only discredits the Russian Supply Commission in the eyes of American Manufacturers....[23]

It is clear from the minutes that the British members were also surprised by the action of their government.

By the June 11, 1917, meeting, the situation for the Russian Supply Commission had grown worse. In early June, the British government formally informed the commission that no additional financial guarantees would be made. The Russian members of the sub-committee presented a written protest to their British counterparts, explaining that the British decision affected "orders which have already been placed ... with American firms on the grounds of information received about the allotment of credits by the British Treasury." The British members replied that, due to the American declaration of war, "the British Government was not, insofar as the British members knew, now at liberty to make independent financial arrangements in America."[24]

Not only was the protest to no avail, but the British government also expanded its decision beyond the refusal to finance new or pending orders. In July 1917, it informed the Russian representatives in London of Britain's "categorical refusal ... to continue payment on Russian orders in the United States in view of the fact that the British Government itself disposes of no other credits in dollars save those which opened for payment of English orders." As a result the Russians requested from the Americans an additional $25 million to cover purchases coming due in America in the immediate future.[25] The Russians later expanded their request to cover all contracts previously placed through Britain, J. P. Morgan and Company or the Russian Supply Commission in America, requesting that an estimated $250 million in debt be transferred from British to Russian liability and funded from American loans. This sudden change was the result of British statements that it could "get American credit only for supplies furnished to herself." Considering that Russia had expressly asked that such a transfer not occur two months earlier, the Americans were not initially obliging. As Ambassador Francis informed the Russian minister of foreign affairs, "England assumed such obligations before we entered the war and before knowing we would enter."[26] Within a short time, Francis conceded that "from a commercial viewpoint England should guarantee such obligations but [it] would be impolitic to so require."[27]

The insistent British effort to unload its Russian obligations was driven by the tenuous state of British finances by mid-1917. On July 1, the British embassy had informed the secretary of state in unusually blunt language of the "urgent and critical" financial position of Britain:

> ...the United States Treasury do not realize how perilous the situation truly is—namely that there is danger that the ability of His Majesty's Government to effect payments in America from today onwards will be in jeopardy. The effect which will be produced on the progress of the war by a collapse of the exchange will be no less disastrous than a great military reverse....[28]

Recalling that Britain had financially supported the Allies for the past three years, the embassy pointed out that Britain had:

> ...discussed the matter thoroughly with the United States Government and ... with the full understanding that they would relieve His Majesty's Government definitely of the expenditure, in the United States, of the other Allied Powers calculating from the day on which the United States entered the war. Up to the present time however His Majesty's Government have borne Russia's entire expenditure in the United States amounting to some $50,000,000 and they have not been informed that this sum will be repaid.

As a result, the British government requested that the first American loans to Russia be charged the amount that it had already spent on Russia's behalf since April, and that money be transferred to Britain.

Bakhmeteff, meanwhile, was wasting no time making his case to the Americans. He had traveled to Massachusetts for a July 22 audience with Colonel Edward House, Wilson's advisor. There, House reported to the president, Bakhmeteff had conceded that Arkhangel'sk would shortly close for the winter and that "Vladivostok is congested and it will take eight months to haul what it [is] now there." For the Russian ambassador, however, these transportation difficulties argued for Russia's urgent need for railroad equipment in the east. Above all else, Bakhmeteff emphasized to House that Russia needed more money from the Americans. The sums yet received from the United States were:

> ...entirely out of proportion to what has been given the other Allies and out of proportion to Russia's great needs. Unless money can be had he believes the [Provisional] Government cannot last. With it ... conditions will steadily improve and a stable democracy will be established.[29]

The British government weighed in on the discussion during the beginning of August, when the British ambassador to the United States outlined for his less experienced Allies the difficulties of dealing with Russian orders. The central problem, he explained, was "the narrow limits within which shipment is possible although ... orders might be placed to an unlimited extent." Vladivostok had an accumulation of 662,000 tons of supplies that would take through the end of 1917 and most of 1918 to move. The British had thus suspended shipments to the port, with the exception of railroad equipment that might expedite the handling of supplies. The White Sea routes would close for the 1917 season with 188,043 tons of unshipped goods left in France; 75,800 tons in Britain and 447,359 tons in the United States.

> The goods which Russia has thus ordered already exceed more than can be shipped by June of next year. Particularly this is the case as far as regards America where at the end of the season enormous masses of material will still remain unshipped.
>
> From the above it follows that it will be useless, for many months to come, to place any more substantial orders for Russia....

Thus, the ambassador concluded that the Russian request for credit for additional orders was totally unreasonable. "...If, however, [the Russian government] were to present such a demand to an inter–Allied council sitting in London it would be impossible for the other Allies to criticize it as unreasonable, seeing as they would be all putting forward demands of their own."[30]

Beyond financial issues, American belligerency permitted the somewhat furtive cooperation between the Russian Commission and British Secret Service to become open. The British Secret Service had a large and active presence in the United States prior to the war, primarily to protect munitions activities, but it had no official standing. With American belligerency, U.S. law enforcement agencies, previously wedded to neutrality, could participate with Allied agencies already working in the country to protect Allied interests. Thus, when the *New York Tribune* in October 1917 published a three-day series of articles attacking the Russian Supply Committee as slackers on security and dupes of German agents, the redoubtable Medzikhovsky could reply with affidavits from both the U.S. and British Secret Services disputing the stories. The *Tribune* alleged that the S.S. *Baron Driesen* had been sabotaged while loading munitions at the Russian Pier in Brooklyn. The device had detonated while the vessel was in port in Arkhangel'sk, destroying a number of other ships.[31] The next day, under the headline "Germans Learned Russian Secrets at Orgies Here," the *Tribune* described wild parties aboard Russian merchant vessels in Brooklyn where "strong drink and the wiles of women vied with each other in loosening the tongues of Russian munitions transportation officials."[32] Finally, the *Tribune* described a thriving trade in liquor smuggling aboard Russian merchant vessels.[33] In May, Lieutenant Francis Kirby, representing the British Secret Service, had surveyed the conditions at the Russian munitions loading pier and found the protective measures in place "excellent."[34] In August the U.S. Secret Service had investigated a number of the charges that formed the basis for the *Tribune* articles. The investigator concluded that "most of the affidavit makers have either been discharged from Russian service or have been in some kind of trouble," while the security firm against which the charges were made had "none but the best of reputations."[35] Faced with a public relations problem, Medzikhovsky found the logical answer in his Tsarist experiences, providing both reports to the Department of State along with a request that the department require that a retraction be printed in the *Tribune*. More plausibly, and chillingly, Medzikhovsky requested that the former employee primarily responsible for the charges "be interned for the duration of the war under the Enemy Trading Act for Action inimical to the United States or her Allies."[36]

7

Bolshevik Revolution and Closure

If British confidence in the Russian cause was eroding, American support received a boost in August with the report of the Root Mission to Russia. Lead by Republican Senator Elihu Root, the mission concluded that, with regard to

> "the policy of giving substantial aid to Russia ... both in supplies and in credits, ... with such aid there is a strong probability of keeping Russia in the war and the Russian Army in the field until a general peace can be made ... there is little prospect that Russia can be kept in the war and the Russian Army in the field without such aid.[1]

The October Revolution put an end to such discussions. As the news of the Bolshevik uprising reached the Allies, even the most sanguine observers of the Russian situation realized the end was at hand. Colonel House, Wilson's trusted advisor, cabled that "in Great Britain the Russian situation is considered at the moment hopeless. There is no responsible government within sight. I would advise making no more advances at present or permitting any further contracts for purchases."[2]

The British, jealous of their own finances, quickly went beyond ending further investment in the Russian war effort. A November 30, 1917, decision of the British War Council not only suspended military aid to Russia, but also directed that existing contracts be converted to Allied use.[3] The British liaisons in America became entirely concerned with liquidating outstanding British-held contracts for Russia, and the Anglo-Russian Sub-Committee became a venue for Russian approval of British contract dispositions. At the December 24, 1917, meeting, the sub-committee authorized the liquidation of the outstanding Westinghouse rifle contracts, recommended offering a specialized storage plant for explosives for sale to the United States government, authorized General Electric to destroy seventy-five rejected shells still held from a contract and settled a $7.12 bill for freight on empty powder boxes.[4]

The liquidation of the Westinghouse rifles contracts ultimately became a lengthy project for the British government. The supplemental contract of May 1, 1917, had provided options on additional rifle production, the first of which came due on September 1. The British government had no interest in ordering more rifles, but the Russians, in the person of Ambassador Bakhmeteff, had convinced the British that they could finance the additional rifles from American credits. When the decision was made to liquidate the arrangement, the simplest and most financially sound course for the British would have been for the company's assets to have been sold piecemeal in the normal fashion. However, the United States government was interested in securing the factories for its own use and entered into a complicated arrangement with Westinghouse and the British where the manufacture of Russian rifles would continue at American expense until the plants could be converted to produce American weapons. As late as January 1919, the British and American governments would still be negotiating the amounts due for this transaction.[5] When production finally ceased, Westinghouse had provided the Russian government with 1,081,490 rifles at a cost of almost $40,000,000 to the British government.[6]

On February 8, 1918, Ambassador Francis cabled Washington with the news that the:

> Central Executive Soviet Committee has approved decree of Council of Commissaries canceling all state loans and all guarantees concluded by the previous government, stating explicitly, "Absolutely and without exception all foreign loans are annulled."[7]

The diplomatic corps in Petrograd immediately issued a collective declaration declining to recognize Soviet authority to seize property or repudiate financial obligations.[8] The Finance Section of the Inter-Allied Council cited the 1831 Diplomatic Conference of London in its statement refusing to recognize the repudiation.[9] Effectively, however, the Allies and the new Russian leadership were speaking different languages. As Francis wrote, the protests of the Petrograd diplomatic corps were answered by statements "charging capitalism waging imperialistic war on proletariat and calling on the workmen of world to unite in opposition."[10]

Even before the Soviet government's February repudiation of Russian debts, the Wilson administration had been struggling to formulate a policy towards the new authority. In the confusion immediately after the October Revolution, the United States had refused to recognize Soviet power. Ambassador Bakhmeteff also refused the legitimacy of the new regime but maintained himself as the recognized Russian ambassador.

Even as Bakhmeteff clung to legitimacy, President Wilson sought outside advice on the Russian situation. On December 8, Lincoln Colcord sent the president a letter based on several weeks of close contact with the Russian ambassador. In it, he advised the president that Bakhmeteff:

> ...knows both Lenine and Trotsky personally, Lenine better than Trotsky. He tells me that Lenine has a simple mind, but a powerful and dogged character. Trotsky is more the theorist, a better thinker than Lenine, frankly an anarchist, and an effective orator.

Though himself a radical, Bakhmeteff was "not ready to admit the deep significance that ... that Lenine and Trotsky, the anarchists, the wild and wrong, have struck the first blow...." As for Bakhmeteff himself:

> He is wonderfully sympathetic towards the lowly people of Russia, but he is not one of them himself. He has been a member of revolutionary societies in his student days under the old regime, yet his family belonged to the bourgeoisie. He has suffered only for freedom, never for bread."[11]

The Allies had been dealing with the military results of the Russian withdrawal from the war since the previous fall. In the face of Soviet intransigence, the Russian financial situation quickly became a question of damage control. By March, the U.S. State Department had requested Treasury provide an account of the current Russian financial obligations in the United States. Treasury primarily relied on information from Serge Ughet, the Russian financial attaché. In the resulting letter, the Treasury observed that:

> the British Government, with the consent of the Anglo-Russian subcommittee, is disposing of all of the materials which were purchased through Morgan's with British funds and applying the proceeds in reduction of Russian obligations held by Great Britain. It would seem, therefore, that the British Government is looking after its interests very well in this respect....[12]

While Treasury was correct about the British, it was also several months behind the times. The liquidation which the British had begun in December 1917 was virtually complete, and the Anglo-Russian Sub-Committee would hold its final meeting on March 15, 1918.[13] On May 5, 1918, the Pekosnarm representatives, still settling outstanding locomotive orders, received a telegram from Petrograd stating that:

> from February nineteen Committee is subject to Soviet Narodnava Khosiaistava Sievernavo Raiona [People's Economic Council, Northern District]. As military orders are finished Commission is herewith asked to store new locomotives, settle accounts with firms, return to Russia.[14]

The Russian Government Commission in London was dissolved on May 31, 1918, and its accounts were turned over to a Russian Liquidation Committee within the *Commission Internationale de Ravitaillement*. Some former members of the Russian Government Commission retained employment with the liquidation committee.[15]

The handling of the liquidation of American railroad orders was a source of friction within the Russian mission. Professor Lomonosov, a professional railway manager of more radical political tendencies, sought to continue the delivery of what he saw as much needed railroad equipment to Russia. Ambassador Bakhmeteff, charged with the closure of the ongoing supply efforts, sought to terminate the contracts and use the completed equipment against its outstanding financial liabilities. Lomonosov ultimately broke from the Russian mission and was denounced by Bakhmeteff after speaking before a pro–Bolshevik rally held at Madison Square Garden on June 11, 1918. He would return to Russia and assume a post in the Soviet government's People's Commissariat of Ways and Communications.[16]

The Americans seemed less anxious than the British to resolve the status of Russian funds in the United States. In part, the Americans were not as financially vulnerable as the British and could afford to let a large account go unused for a time. They also were not fatigued by several years of unfruitful dealings with Russian representatives. But perhaps most critically, the Russian representatives in the United States could still be valuable to American foreign policy.

A very real concern in the days prior to the landings of American and British forces on the Murman Coast, however, was the enormous quantity of military supplies that Russian transport had left stockpiled at Arkhangel'sk, Murmansk and also at Vladivostok. The material at Vladivostok alone was estimated at 700,000 to 750,000 tons and valued at as much as $1 billion.[17] By February 1918, Arkhangel'sk was in Bolshevik hands, and supplies were being removed.[18] The most benign hope was that these supplies would be used to support Bolshevik operations. In the fluid politics of revolutionary Russia, the prospect of these supplies falling into German hands could not be discounted.

The initial Allied effort to deny war supplies to Germany ultimately expanded into an attempt to strangle the Bolshevik regime. The Russian representatives remaining in the United States had an interest in aiding the various White Armies, and the United States government both tolerated and encouraged their activities. The settlement of the British orders left the Russians still in possession of a number of contracts for military goods that could be routed to the anti–Bolshevik forces. An inventory of Russian Supply Commission assets from May 1, 1918, indicated that the committee still controlled $167,825,425 in supplies. At the height of the effort, the Russians were even purchasing additional supplies from contracts that the United States after the Armistice no longer needed. At least two ships of the Russian Volunteer Fleet delivered American goods to Denikin's forces in mid–1919, while at least four more shipments reached him between September and November 1919. All told, approximately $77 million in Russian Supply Commission assets were transferred to the White cause.[19]

With the American and British governments accounting for three years of large-scale spending, a former member of the Russian Supply Commission in America attempted an accounting of a different nature. In late 1918, Moisei I. Gaiduk published a volume whose title translated as *The Flatiron: Material and Facts about the Supply Activities of the Russia Military Commission in America*. While only employed by the commission for a year, probably spanning 1917 and 1918, Gaiduk had worked in the Artillery Commission, the Anglo-Russian Sub-Committee and the Liquidation Commission.[20] Written in his native Russian, the volume was published by Ivan K. Okuntsov, the editor of *Russkii Golos* ("The Russian Voice"), a New York City Russian language newspaper. Okuntsov was a socialist, arrested and sentenced to death for revolutionary activity in February 1906. Escaping to the United States, he founded *Russkii Golos* in October 1907. While other socialist immigrants accused him of softening his politics in the intervening years, Gaiduk's book presented an opportunity to present the ineptitude and waste of the Tsarist and Provisional Governments through first-hand testimony.[21] Whatever the politics behind it, Gaiduk carefully buttressed his case by reproducing verbatim documents from the commission; minutes of meetings, speeches, and personal correspondence. In a number of cases, the original documents are available through archival sources and confirm the fidelity of Gaiduk's reproduction. He also recounts a number of anecdotes, distinguishing between those he was told during his employment and those he experienced. The result is a unique and valuable account.

Given the amount of assistance that the vestiges of the Russian supply effort were providing the White forces, the new regime had to take some kind of action. In spring, 1919, the ambassador for the Provisional Government received a most unwelcome letter, imprinted:

Russian Socialist Federal Soviet Republic

Bureau of the Representative in the United States of America

On it, the new aspirant to replace Ambassador Bakhmeteff, Ludwig. A. Martens, officially presented his authority as the Soviet representative:

> In behalf of the Russian Socialist Federal Soviet Republics and as the duly accredited representative of the said Government in the United States, I hereby command you to turn over to me immediately upon receipt hereof all property of the Russian Government in your possession or under your control, including the Embassy Building at Washington, D. C. ... all property of the former Russian Railways Mission and Supplies Committee....

As for Bakhmeteff himself:

> ...your post of Russian Ambassador to the United States became vacant and your rights and title ... were legally terminated with the overthrow of the Government....
>
> On behalf of said Russian Socialist Federal Soviet Republic I claim that the said Government is the only existing Government in Russia, de jure and de facto; that the Government whom you alleged to represent in this country has absolutely gone out of existence on the 6th day of November, 1917; that there is not at this time even the barest pretense of its power or existence....
>
> The workers and peasants of Russia and their government have learned with deep indignation and just wrath that you, together with an array of idle former officials ... representing nobody but yourself and a small clique

of former exploiters of Russia, are using funds and property belonging to the Russian people ... for purposes openly hostile to the Russian people. ... if you disregard this notice you will do so at your own peril.[22]

Martens had sent his diplomatic credentials to the Department of State on March 18. Enclosed was a lengthy explanation of what the Soviet government viewed as its unique source of legitimacy and a proposal for renewed trade. Forwarding the news to the Secretary of State, then in Paris for the Versailles Conference, the department commented on:

the ingeniousness of the proposal of the Bolshevik representative to deposit $200,000,000 in gold in the United States and Allied countries, when the government he represents has repudiated the enormous foreign debts of Russia, including $187,000,000 advanced by the United States....[23]

The department also commented that Martens' presentation of credentials had been widely reported in the press and offered a clear opportunity to declare publicly American policy towards "a regime whose Constitution ... stipulates that among its fundamental tasks are the securing of the victory of Socialism in all countries, the abolition of private property, the repudiation of foreign obligations, and the complete elimination of whole classes from ... Government."[24]

Not content to wait for American reaction, Martens had sent his notice to the embassy, and followed it with direct communications to private firms that were doing business with the Provisional Government. At the National City Bank of New York, a major financial broker for the Russian government, Martens presented his credentials and informed the bank that all Russian funds were now under the control of the Bolshevik authorities.[25] The Coudert Brothers, attorneys for various Russian supply interests, received a letter from Martens claiming title to any Russian property under their control. The Soviet representative attached a copy of his letter to Bakhmeteff, and warned that "Any disposition which you may make ... of the said property pending an authoritative ajuducation [*sic*] will be made upon your own responsibility."[26]

Taking the direct approach, the law firm addressed the question to the Department of State. The reply was dated a mere five days later. The acting secretary indicated that:

In a recent telegram ... [the Secretary of State] states that the only Russian representative recognized by the United States is Mr. Bakhmeteff, and adds in effect that the claims to a representative capacity put forth by Mr. L. A. Martens are not to be given credence. I may add that the

> Government of the United States has not received nor recognized Mr. Martens in any representative capacity ... and moreover that the Department has received no authentic evidence that Mr. Martens is even the representative in the United States of the so-called "Russian Socialist Federal Soviet Republics." As you are no doubt aware, this Government has never recognized the Bolshevik regime as a Government either de facto or de jure.[27]

The National City Bank received a similar reply from the department, and hastened to seek assurances that "any recognition of the present Soviet Administration ... [would] apply only to future relations and transactions ... to avoid the possibility that the recognition may have a retroactive effect."[28] The acting secretary replied that, while "there is no question" of recognition of Soviet authority, "any recognition hereafter accorded will not have any retroactive effect ... prejudicial to American interests."[29] National City could continue as Russia's bankers without fear of later liability.

Perhaps the crowning irony in the Martens affair came later in June 1919, as the United States government began efforts to intern the Soviet representative as an undesirable alien. According to the senior State Department analyst for Russian affairs, Martens had been born in Russia of German parents, and had long ties to Russian radical groups. After the 1905 Revolution, he fled to Britain, where he worked as an engineer. "He came to the U.S. in 1916 as a representative of the Demidoffs—big munitions makers in Russia."[30]

On April 28, 1922, Bakhmeteff informed the Secretary of State that, for personal reasons, he would soon be departing the United States. As "my status as Ambassador has been made the subject of renewed discussion," he offered to "terminate ... official functions."[31] In reply, Secretary Hughes observed that:

> inasmuch as the liquidation and final settlement of the business of the Russian Government in the United States for which you were responsible is now practically completed ... your continuance as Ambassador under the existing circumstances may give rise to misunderstanding.[32]

Bakhmeteff's status as the Russian ambassador to the United States, and the last vestige of the Russian Supply Commission expired on June 30, 1922. Bakhmeteff returned to his trade and in 1931 became a professor of civil engineering at Columbia University.[33]

Lieutenant Boris Brasol, the former Petrograd prosecutor turned supply commission investigator, pursued a more controversial course. By

December 1917, he left Russian government service and became an employee of the United States government, serving as a translator for the War Trade Board, and later, by his own account, as an advisor to the chief the U.S. Army Military Intelligence Bureau.[34] His real vocation, however, was anti–Bolshevism and he was closely connected to prominent White Russian circles. He was dissatisfied with the Russian embassy's handling of the "considerable funds" he believed it had available for anti–Bolshevik work:

> ...Russian organizations and individuals have approached the Russian Embassy with the request to make an organized effort to promote loyal Russian propaganda in the United States. Every time we have met with rabid opposition on the part of the Embassy ... Mr. Bakhmeteff simply would not listen to any suggestion as long as they did not coincide with his Jewish tendencies. Therefore, it was soon found necessary to drop further negotiations with the so-called Russian officials and to try to work out something dependent entirely upon individual efforts....[35]

Between 1920 and 1922, he wrote a series of books asserting the failure and illegitimacy of the Soviet government.[36]

Brasol was convinced that Bolshevism had been "imposed on her [Russia] by a gang of Jewish internationalists" and his anti–Semitism and anti–Bolshevism became essentially indistinguishable.[37] For a brief time, Brasol became a figure of some public notoriety, and the series of allegations made against him in the press is difficult if not impossible to prove or disprove. He was attacked as an Okhrana agent, and it was alleged that he been a prosecutor at the 1913 Beilis trial and had been the original translator of the *Protocols of the Elders of Zion*, a notorious anti–Semitic forgery, into English.[38] The truth is probably more mundane. A virulent anti–Semite, Brasol used his belief to find common cause with anyone he thought might help liberate Russia. Ultimately, in the 1930s and 1940s, this search would lead him to associate with the Klu Klux Klan and a number of "America First" and American fascist organizations.[39]

Brasol concealed his beliefs under a persona of culture and considerable legal talent. In 1927, Oxford University Press published his book *The Elements of Crime (Psycho-Social Interpretation)* and Columbia University employed him in a survey of criminological research. Later in life, he authored a book on Oscar Wilde, and translated Pushkin and Dostoievsky. In 1933 Brasol's attitudes became the centerpiece of a legal battle between the United States and the Soviet governments over the remains of the wartime Russian supply efforts. In 1917, the United States government had requisitioned two partially completed ships of the Russian Volunteer Fleet, a body that had done much work for the supply commission. The October Revolution occurred before payment was made for the ships, and the United States declined to settle with the Soviets. Filed in 1923, the suit dragged on for ten years before coming to trial. The Soviet representative argued that the Russian Volunteer Fleet was a corporation and entitled to receive the $5 million owed for the ships. The United States sought to establish that the fleet was an instrument of the Russian government and thus ceased to exist with the revolution. As its expert witness on Russian law and government, the United States called Brasol. His legal background and experience with the supply commission should have made him the ideal witness in the matter. Much of his six days of testimony, however, consisted of cross-examination by the lawyer representing the Soviets concerning his anti–Semitic and anti–Soviet activities, with the Soviets arguing that he could not be an objective witness. Thus, the United States attorney was left defending Brasol's reputation and veracity.[40]

While the question of where the Russian assets in the United States and Britain went after the war remains open, it is clear that no real part of them wound up in the hands of General Hermonious. After the war, the general settled in Paris as part of the distinguished but financially destitute Russian émigré community. In 1922, Hermonious wrote Stettinius soliciting a $5,000 investment to establish a business producing knit clothes using automatic knitting machines. Hermonious had been one of the few Russian officials for whom the Morgan partner felt any respect, and Hermonious received his money. Hermonious' business effort ultimately failed. In early 1923, Stettinius wrote one of the Morgan representatives in Paris:

> There is something very pitiful about the old man's [Hermonious'] letter and I am afraid that he is in pretty bad shape. If he calls on you, please give him the benefit of any advice that you think may be helpful. Incidentally, do not hesitate to give him for my account any reasonable amount you may find he requires. I should doubt the wisdom of giving him any large amounts, say up to $1,000, and imagine it would be better to dole out say, up to this amount in small sums....[41]

After the war, as during, the Allies still felt Russia was a charity case.

8

Conclusion

Within the nation-state system, the first imperative for state legitimacy is the ability to hold and defend territory. To that end states dedicate treasure, personnel and at least a modicum of professional competence to their military organs. In struggles for national survival, the industrial warfare that has marked the twentieth century has demanded the complete resources of the nations involved. In Imperial Russia, both the government and civil society failed the test represented by the First World War.

As the bureaucracy moved to meet Russian supply requirements, the autocratic nature of authority in Russia and the resulting ministerial fragmentation handicapped its efforts. With power invested entirely in the person of the tsar, the state bureaucracy could never be permitted a position, whether held by a ministry, council or a single individual, entrusted with real executive authority. Thus it was that the extent of the Russian supply problem was poorly understood in government circles—no single organ had the responsibility to assess supply requirements, much less coordinate their fulfillment. The conflicting Russian assessments of their own supply needs which confused and frustrated the Allies were as much a result of this institutional failing as any effort to deceive. One effect of this system was that the British government probably developed a better overall understanding of the Russian supply system than the individual Russian ministries. British representatives could gather information from across agencies, inside and outside of Russia, to assemble a comprehensive picture of the problem.

When the bureaucracy did address supply problems, the ministerial system allowed no mechanism to allocate resources in a rational, prioritized manner. Russian purchasing was restricted by the limited capital available, be it from Russian foreign exchange or Allied loans; by the number of foreign manufacturers able to produce munitions and specialized goods; and by the simple mathematics of merchant shipping tonnage and rail capacity. In 1914, the new and unfamiliar nature of large overseas orders probably caused these factors to be overlooked; by 1916, they were simply being ignored. The Ministry of Commerce worked diligently through 1916 and 1917 to purchase railroad equipment that the Finance Ministry could ill afford and that probably could not be shipped to Russia, much less to the Russian interior. The ability of the British government to approach the *Stavka* directly in 1915 became the genesis of the special supply relationship between Grand Duke Nicholas and Lord Kitchener. The same disorder that permitted this effort, however, made considered agreements between the Allies only imperfectly binding on the Russian bureaucracy. Even given a perfect system, Russian supply would have presented difficult choices and daunting challenges. Yet trapped by institutional attitudes poorly fitted to the task, the Russian bureaucracy exacerbated the already difficult situation.

The implementation of the special councils in 1915 failed to rectify this problem. The government never truly intended these organs to become a means of inter-ministry coordination. Rather, in the eyes of the government, the special councils were a means of pacifying the liberal elements in the Duma after the shell crisis. Meetings with the opposition, however loyal, could not be an effective venue for coordination between ministries. No minister would entertain airing specific grievances in such a forum.

The failure of the autocratic Tsarist government to organize becomes more ironic when contrasted with the measures taken by the other, largely democratic, belligerents. Both Britain and France created munitions ministries with sweeping powers over the economy. Imperial Germany attempted to militarize in their entirety key supply sectors of the economy. Even the traditionally non-interventionist United States created a War Industries Board which created standards for production and nationalized the rail system.

As an organizing force in Russian military supply, the major non-governmental organizations also failed. Their reception overseas makes it clear that the liberals who made up the leadership of the zemstvo movement and the industrialists who led the War-Industries Committees were politically more attuned to the Allies than their government counterparts. It does not follow that they were institutionally or individually better equipped to deal with wartime orders abroad. The difficulties created by Russian management in the American Locomotive Company orders closely mirror those encountered by governmental orders.

The continuance of these difficulties after the installation of the Provisional Government largely belies the assertion that the failure of civil society in foreign purchasing was a result of Tsarist government policies. Further, the non-governmental organizations working abroad enjoyed considerable freedom, even after the government sought to restrict their efforts as the war progressed.

Ironically, the sincere distrust civil society held toward the government and political opportunism combined to obstruct some government moves towards increased supply effectiveness. Immediately after the industrial congress had authorized the Central Committee, the Moscow Zemstvo passed a resolution in favor of complete state control of industry. The opinion was echoed by other district zemstvos. In response, *Utro Russii* (Russian Morning), a pro-industrial newspaper, commented:

> The zemstvos have attempted to deliver public initiative into the hands of those very elements whose inability to deal with the great problem of national defense has been proved. It is this incompetence that has caused the present unanimous desire of all the productive forces of Russia to come to the aid of our heroic armies.[1]

Within the voluntary associations, the leadership was acutely aware of the government's failing and their own importance to the continuation of the war and the regime. Prince Lvov, in a March 1916 speech to an assembly of zemstvo delegates stated:

> The Fatherland is in danger.... The Regime is not guiding the ship of state ... [nevertheless] the ship is holding steadily to its course, and work aboard has not stopped. The ship's crew is preserving order and self-control. We shall not stop, and we shall not fall into confusion.[2]

But for all Lvov's optimism, no voluntary society was a sufficient replacement for an active and effective government. With the terrible demands of war weighing on every aspect of the society, where the Imperial government would not offer the guidance the Russian ship of state needed, civil society could not. Standing before the Duma on November 1, 1916, Miliukov asked his fellow delegates:

> when the Duma with ever greater persistence insists that the rear must be organized for a successful struggle, which the government persists in claiming that organizing the country means organizing a revolution and deliberately prefers chaos and disorganization, then what is this: stupidity or treason?[3]

At that instant, the answer hardly mattered. Rather, he said Russians should:

> forget further attempts to harmonize your work jointly with the present authorities; they are doomed to failure, they only separate us from our goal. Do not succumb to illusions; turn away from phantoms! There is no authority![4]

Standing in the Tauride Palace that day, what Miliukov could not see from his proximity was that Russia would follow his injunction and abandon the "present authorities." What he did not see was that the failure of authority included himself, the Duma and the new national organizations. In their place, the people would install their own representatives.

Speaking at a distance of almost a decade, Ambassador Bakhmeteff put it more simply:

> The social eruption, as it befell Russia, was a direct consequence of the War. The people entered the struggle in high spirits, full of patriotic enthusiasm. For over two years they carried on with rare courage and tenacity, against the odds of inadequate munitions, inefficient military command, and, most of all, a sinister confusion reigning around the throne. The strain proved to be too great. Exhausted, disheartened, the nation lost morale, faith, and broke down in tragic convulsions.[5]
>
> My generation was in the sweep of the avalanche.[6]

Appendix A

Chronology of Events Relating to Russian Supply with Major Wartime Events

1914

July 26	Duma meets for one-day session, creates "*union sacrée*"
July 30	All-Russian Union of Zemstvos meets in Moscow
July 31	Russia orders general mobilization
August 1	Germany declares war on Russia
August 4	Britain declares war on Germany
September 14	Russian defeat in the Battle of Tannenberg
September 27	*Commission Internationale de Ravitaillement* (CIR) holds first meeting of the Anglo-Russian Committee of Supply
October 23	President Wilson authorizes commercial credits for belligerent nations
October 29	Turkey closes the Dardanelles to Russian commerce

1915

January	Russian Government Committee in London established
January 15	J. P. Morgan and Company becomes British purchasing agent in the United States
January 24	Russia signs contract for one million rifles with Remington Arms
January	Duma recalled for three day session
February 4–5	Conference of Allied Financial Ministers in Paris, British propose coordinating war orders in America
May	Reports of ammunition shortages on the Western Front begin British "shell crisis"; Russians retreat from Galicia, blaming inadequate munitions
May	Colonel Ellershaw visits the *Stavka*, Grand Duke Nicholas appoints Kitchener as his agent for munitions
May 3	J. P. Morgan and Company becomes French purchasing agent in the United States
May 7	*Lusitania* sunk
May 19	First "Special Council" to superintend supply formed by Tsarist decree
June	Ninth All-Russian Congress of the Association of Industry and Trade establishes Central War-Industries Committee
June 7	Special Council revised
June 9	Britain establishes Ministry of Munitions
July	General Hermonius, Colonel Ellershaw visit United States to inspect Russian supply efforts
July 31	Duma resumes session
September 3	Duma is suspended
September 8	Grand Duke Nicholas is dismissed, Tsar Nicholas II takes personal command of Russian forces
September 30	Anglo-Russian agreement calls for formation of Russian Supply Commission in America (RSC)
October 13	First meeting of RSC held in New York
November 19	RSC approves formal rules for contracts
November 23	Inter-Allied Munitions Conference held in London

1916

January 1	Edward Stettinius Sr. made partner in J. P. Morgan and Company

April	General F. F. Minchin is appointed to head British supply inspection in the United States
May 5	Anglo-Russian transportation agreement
June	Russia begins Brusilov offensive in Galicia
June 5	Lord Kitchener and Colonel Ellershaw die when the cruiser *Hampshire* hits a mine and sinks en route to Russia
July 14	Anglo-Russian Conference in London establishes Anglo-Russian Sub-Committee of the RSC
July 30	Explosion at Black Tom Port Facility, New Jersey
August 25	General Zaluboffsky replaces General Sapojnikov as head of RSC
November	General Minchin is appointed full-time British representative to the Anglo-Russian Sub-Committee
November 1	Duma recalled
November 8–10	Inter-Allied Supply Conference held in London

1917

January 11	Explosion at Kingsland, New Jersey, munitions factory
March	February revolution
March 15	Tsar Nicholas II abdicates
March 20	United States recognizes Provisional Government
April 6	United States declares war on Germany
June	Britain ends financial guarantee of future Russian contracts in U.S.
July	Britain ends payments on outstanding Russian orders in U.S.
July	Bakhmeteff arrives in United States as ambassador, General Khrabrov relieves General Zaluboffsky as head of RSC
August 24	Russian agreement consolidates approval for purchasing in U.S. under U.S. War Industries Board
September 1	J. P. Morgan and Company ceases representing Allies for purchasing matters
November	Bolshevik revolution in Petrograd
November 24	Colonel House, advisor to President Wilson, advises no further Russian contracts be permitted
November 30	Britain directs outstanding Russian contracts be converted to Allied use

1918

March 3	The Bolshevik government signs the Treaty of Brest-Litovsk
May 5	Final meeting of the Anglo-Russian Sub-Committee of the RSC
May 31	Russian Government Commission in London dissolved
June 23	In the first Allied intervention, British forces land at Murmansk, in part to secure the large amount of imported supplies built up during the war
July 16	Tsar and family executed
November 11	Armistice ends combat

1919

January 18	The Versailles Peace Conference begins

1920

January 21	Admiral Kolchak executed by Bolsheviks

1922

April 28	Boris Bakhmeteff resigns as Russian ambassador to the United States effective June 30

Appendix B

Procedure to Be Pursued for the Purchase of Machine Tools for Russia in America*

1. All requirements will be submitted in the first instance to the Commission Internationale in London through the Russian Government Committee in London and will not be sent to the Russian Commission in America.
2. The Commission Internationale will submit all these requirements to the Machine Tool Department of the Ministry of Munitions.
3. The Machine Tool Department will decide whether the requirements can be fulfilled in this country, and if so, will obtain quotations for the information and approval of the Russian Delegation on the Commission Internationale. On hearing from the Commission Internationale that the quotations are approved the Machine Tool Department will place the order through the Contracts Department

*RG 261, *Records of the Agent of Trade and Industry, "Procedure to be used for the purchase of machine tools for Russia in America."*

of the Ministry of Munitions. It is understood that the Commission Internationale will be responsible that credits are available. The Finance Department of the ministry will be advised by the Contracts Department that these orders have been placed that the necessary financial records can be kept. The Commission Internationale must also be informed of contracts as they are placed.

4. Any orders which the Machine Tool Department is unable to place in this country may be dealt with in either of the following ways according to the circumstances of each case:
   (a). They may be orders in America through Morgan who, after consultation with Searle, will buy the machine tools under the direct instructions of the Ministry. Morgans will sign the contract and make the payments and their London house will communicate with the Finance Department of the Ministry so that proper financial records may be kept. They will also notify their purchases to the Russian Committee in America. In these circumstances the Machine Tool Department must receive from the Commission Internationale complete instructions regarding shipment and identification marks so that Morgans may be properly instructed.
   (b). The Machine Tool Department may refer these orders back to the Commission Internationale with an intimation that the Machine Tool Department cannot deal with these orders. In this event the Commission Internationale will inform the Russian Government Committee, who will, if they desire it, place the orders elsewhere. Should the Russian Government Committee desire to place the orders in America they will notify the Russian Commission in America. The Commission has agreed to ask the Conference or Sub-Committee of which Mr. Searle is a member to negotiate the orders.

In this case Morgans will not sign the contracts which will be signed by the Russian Commission or Sub-Committee of which Searle is a member, as may be directed by the Chairman of the Russian Commission. Searle will, through Morgans, cable Morgans London house for direct transmission to the Commission Internationale particulars of all contracts which he proposes to approve, or if the matter is urgent, of the contract which has been placed. It is understood that the Ministry of Munitions takes no responsibility with respect to orders falling under class (b). They lend Searle to the Russian Commission in order that he may act as a member of the Sub-Committee in the interests of the Commission Internationale and of the Treasury.

(signed) Domydoff

Appendix C

Statute Governing the Russian Supply Committee in America*

APPROVED 18/31 MARCH 1916

1. The Russian Supply Committee, in which is to be included a representative of the British Government is inaugurated in the U. S. A. for the purpose of placing orders in America, making purchases there and carrying out other instructions of the Russian Government relating to the Defence of the Realm; as well as for the purpose of assisting in the carrying out of orders placed in America by local organizations and private firms engaged in Russia on War Work.

   NOTE. This Statute does not refer to supplies manufactured in Canada. With reference to the latter supplies the Committee has merely instructions to see that the manufacture and ship-

**RG 261, Records of the Office of the Chairman, "Statute governing the Russian Supply Committee in America."*

ment is duly carried out, with power to exercise the right to control the Agents acting on behalf of the Government in connection with the manufacture to these supplies.

2. The Committee shall act on accordance with the financial Agreements, on the basis of which foreign Credit is placed at the disposal of the Russian Government.
3. The duties of the Committee are as follows:
   (a). To consider offers for supply and manufacture of material and equipment necessary for the Defence of the Realm.
   (b). To place such orders and make such purchases on behalf of the Central Organizations and Departments, or independently, or through the representative of the British Government in America—in accordance with instructions issued by the Russian Government Committee in London in all cases except as provided under Note 3 of this paragraph.

NOTE 1 In the case of orders placed independently by the Committee the concurrence of the representative of the British Government on the Committee with regard to the principal points of the proposed order will obviate the necessity of communicating with the British Government in London.
NOTE 2 In the case of Orders placed by Messrs. Morgan to the instruction of the British Government the principal points of the proposed Contract, as well as the specifications and rules of inspection shall be submitted to the Russian Supply Committee for approval at a special Anglo-Russian Commission meeting of which the following members form the quota:

Two Representatives of the Committee,
the Representative of the British Government, and
the Representative of Messrs. Morgan.

NOTE 3 In the event of the above mentioned orders not being paid for out of Credits placed a the disposal of the Russian Government in accordance with the Financial Agreements, the Committee may carry out the transactions indicated without previously obtaining the approval of the Russian Government Committee in London, but must inform the latter of all such transactions in due course.

(c). To make payments on behalf of the Departments and organizations as well as on the Committee's own orders and purchases.
(d). To ascertain what materials and supplies could be purchased in America, and the conditions on which such purchases could be made.

(e). To furnish information as to the standing of American firms upon enquiries received from the corresponding Russian Government and local organizations.

(f). Supervise the work on War supplies manufactured in America and ordered either independently by the Committee or through the representative of the British Government, and—in case of delays in the furnishing of the supplies—to ascertain and remove the cause of delay, possibly by altering minor details of the specifications without previously consulting the Russian Government Committee in London; to organize the inspection of the ordered supplies and in suitable instances their dispatch to Russia.

(g). To discount the foreign credit, which has been placed at the disposal of the Committee, and to furnish monthly reports to the Commission dealing with the discounting and distribution of foreign credit. (Valuta commission)

4. The Membership of the Committee shall include:

(a). Delegates from the Ministries of War, Marine, Finance, and Trade and Commerce, appointed by the Heads of the corresponding Departments, and also such representatives of the above named Departments whose membership is regarded necessary by the Heads of the Departments and in addition—delegates of the Central War Industries Committee and the Chief Army Supply Committee of the All Russian Zemsky and Town Municipal Union in accordance with the choice of these local organizations. Along with the above delegates, may be included from other departments and institutions as well as Committees inaugurated by the Special Council for the Defence of the Realm—mutually agreed upon by the Minister of War, as President of this special Council, and the corresponding departmental Head;

(b). A Representative of the British Government.

NOTE 1 By special invitation of the President of the Committee, persons whose knowledge and work make their presence desirable may take part in the deliberation of the Committee.
NOTE 2 Military and Naval Officers, sent over to America for the purpose of following up and inspecting supplies are within the bounds of their mission subordinated to the corresponding delegate.

5. At the Head of the committee stands the President of the committee, appointed by the President of the Special Council for the

Defence of the Realm. In case of absence or illness of the President of the Committee, the President of the Special Council appoints a Vice-President, who, when performing the duties of the President acquires the rights of the latter.

6. In matters concerning requirements for the Defence of the Realm the President is subordinate to the Imperial Russian Government in the person of the Minister of War as President of the Special Council for the Defence of the Realm.
7. Questions arising within the jurisdiction of the Committee are entered for discussion at Committee meetings by the President. The resolutions of the Committee are passed on a majority of votes and in the case of an even number for and against the vote of the President shall decide. Should the President disagree with the Resolution passed he shall have the right to enforce his own decision, at the same time bringing this decision to the notice of the President of the Special Council for the Defence of the Realm. In the cases referred to in NOTE 1 of Paragraph 3b. it is necessary that the concurrence of the committee representative of the British Government be obtained to the main conditions of the proposed order.
8. Contracts, Agreements and Powers of Attorney on Committee matters shall be signed by the President and Delegate of the corresponding Department or local organization, or by the latter only—provided he has the President's authority for this—and countersigned by the Secretary of the Committee.
9. At the approach of a date on which payment becomes due on a sanctioned order, the Committee shall inform the Valuta Commission and the Department or local organizations concerned of the necessity for making payment (pointing out the Contract, date on which payment becomes due, place and person to whom payments should be made and the Works). The Commission then informs the "Credit Chancellery" which issues the necessary instructions for payment to be made to the proper person or firm, upon receipt of an assignment from the corresponding institution.

   NOTE payments for Orders of private undertakings or individuals are carried out in the same manner, but instead of an assignment the "Credit Chancellery" receives the corresponding sum of money.

10. The Committee has a right to delegate one or more of its Members for the purpose of transacting business within the jurisdiction of the Committee, each time in accordance with a resolution of the Committee.

11. A Chancellery shall be attached to the Committee and it shall include an accountancy section.
12. Estimates for the expenses of the Committee and the attached Chancellery with its accountancy section furnished by the President is subject to the approval of the President of the special Council for the Defence of the Realm.
13. Committee Expenses (Salaries for the Staff, Secretarial and general expenses, traveling and other expenses) are paid to the order of the President, from the sums specially assigned for that purpose by the President of the Special Council, in agreement with Minister of Finance.
14. The details of the constitution of the Committee shall be determined by the Committee itself.
15. All doubtful points arising out of the interpretation of this Statute shall be settled by the Minister of War as President of the Special Council for the Defence of the Realm.

Appendix D

Agreement Establishing the Anglo-Russian Sub-Committee*

The Government of His Britannic Majesty and the Government of His Majesty the Emperor of Russia, being desirous of securing in the United States of America the better co-ordination of their effort and the acceleration of deliveries on existing contracts for the supply of materials required in the prosecution of the war, have agreed upon the following arrangements:

1. Subsequent to the date of this Agreement all new orders which are to be paid for from credits furnished by the British Government shall be placed in the United States by the Russian Supplies Commission, which Commission shall include two representative of the British Government, who together shall exercise one vote, and no such

**RG 261, Records of the Office of the Chairman, "Agreement establishing the Anglo-Russian Sub-Committee."*

orders shall be placed by the Commission until it has been ascertained by consultation between the Russian Commission in London and the British Government, that the material required cannot be obtained in the United Kingdom or in Canada, or cannot be supplied out of contracts already placed by the British Government. With this object all orders requiring British finance shall in the first instance be transmitted by the Russian Government to the Russian Commission in London, and if it is not possible to obtain what is required in the United Kingdom or in Canada the Russian Commission in London will communicate with His Britannic Majesty's Treasury and obtain from them written assurance that the necessary funds are available before requesting the Commission in New York to place orders in the United States. The Russian Supplies Commission in the United States will employ Messrs. J. P. Morgan and Company for the conduct of all enquiries and negotiations with contractors. Messrs. J. P. Morgan and Company will be entrusted with the drawing up of the necessary contracts; the choice of firms, the specifications, deliveries and all main points of the contracts, including prices being decided by the Commission. Messrs. J. P. Morgan and Company will receive their instructions direct from the Commission. No negotiations relating to orders placed in the United States on behalf of the Russian Government shall be conducted without the knowledge and approval of the Russian Supplies Commission.

2. In accordance with the general intentions expressed in clause (3) Note 2 of the Statutes and Bye-laws of governing the procedure of the Russian Supplies Commission in America, a special Anglo-Russian Sub-Committee shall be constituted forthwith, consisting of four persons, namely, the President and one other member of the Russian Commission in New York, together with two representatives of the British Government, who together shall exercise one vote.

   Subject to the authority of the respective Governments this sub-Committee shall be vested by the Russian Supplies Commission with supreme control of all matters pertaining to the execution of all orders already placed in the United States by the British Government for the Russian Government, and of the order place with the Canadian Car and Foundry Company, including the inspection of deliveries thereunder.

3. Any person whose assistance will be considered useful may be invited to the Conference of the Anglo-Russian Sub-Committee.

4. Every member of the Anglo-Russian Sub-Committee shall have a

Deputy with full authority to act on his behalf in the event of his absence through illness or any other cause.

5. The Russian Inspecting Staff acting under the instructions of their respective Chiefs and under the supreme control of the President of the Russian Supplies Commission shall have complete freedom of action in settling, with the concurrence of the contractors, all questions of a purely technical character. All questions as to the interpretation of contracts which involve the financial liability of the British Government shall be dealt with by the Anglo-Russian Sub-Committee and must be decided unanimously.
6. All decisions of the Anglo-Russian Sub-Committee will be communicated to the Russian Supplies Commission which will forthwith issue the necessary instructions to those whom they may concern.
7. No direct negotiation between the contractors concerned and the British or Russian Governments with regard to orders under the control of the Anglo-Russian Sub-Committee are permissible. Any communications addressed by the contractors to the British or Russian authorities in London or Petrograd shall be forwarded to and dealt with by the Anglo-Russian Sub-Committee in New York.
8. The above arrangements being of an experimental nature may be terminated at any time upon notice being given, in writing, to the parties thereto.

It may be modified at any time by mutual consent.

IN WITNESS WHEREOF the undersigned have signed the present Agreement and have affixed thereto their Seals.

Done at London in duplicate, the fourteenth day of July, 1916.

E. Grey
Benckendorff

Notes

Introduction

1. For example, Paul Miliukov, leader of the Constitutional Democrat ("Kadet") Party and foreign minister of the Provisional Government, was a history professor who had made an extensive speaking tour of the United States and Britain in 1904 and 1905. During the First World War, he traveled to Europe as a representative of the State Duma. After 1917, he lived in exile in France. His 1904–05 lectures were published as *Russia and its Crisis* (Reprint edition; New York: Collier Books, 1962) and his career is detailed in his *Political Memoirs, 1905–1917*, trans. Carl Goldberg (Ann Arbor: University of Michigan Press, 1967).

2. An outstanding example of this phenomenon is the Russian series of the Carnegie Endowment. Published in the 1920s and 1930s by Yale University, this multi-volume set still forms a useful point of departure for research into the effects of the First World War on Russia. The authorship was a virtual who's who of Russian liberals in exile, and included former State Duma members, the mayor of Moscow and zemstvo officials.

3. Theodore H. Von Laue, "The Prospects of Liberal Democracy in Tsarist Russia," in *Essays on Russian Liberalism*, ed. Charles E. Timberlake (Columbia: University of Missouri Press, 1972), 164–65.

4. James Cracraft, "Empire Versus Nation: Russian Political Theory under Peter I," *Harvard Ukrainian Studies* (December 1986): 524–41.

5. Richard Pipes, *Russia under the Old Regime* (New York: Charles Scribners' Sons, 1974), 281–90.

6. Richard G. Robbins, *The Tsar's Viceroys: Russian Provincial Governors in the Last Years of the Empire* (Ithaca, N.Y.: Cornell University Press, 1987), 91–98; Robert B. McKean, *St. Petersburg Between the Revolutions: Workers and Revolutionaries, June 1907– February 1917* (New Haven: Yale University Press, 1990), 286.

7. Jacob Walkin, *The Rise of Democracy in Pre-Revolutionary Russia: Political and Social Institutions Under the Last Three Czars* (New York: Frederick A. Praeger, 1962), 31–33.

8. Michael Hughes, *Diplomacy before the Russian Revolution: Britain, Russia and the Old Diplomacy, 1894–1917* (New York: St. Martin's Press, 2000), 172.

9. Two of the best works in recent years are Mary Schaeffer Conroy, ed. *Emerging Democracy in Late Imperial Russia: Case Studies on Local Self-Government (The Zemstvos), State Duma Elections, the Tsarist Government and the State Council before and during World War I* (Niwot: University Press of Colorado, 1998) and Thomas Earl Porter, *The Zemstvo and the Emergence of Civil Society in Late Imperial Russia, 1864–1917*. Distinguished dissertations series (San Francisco: Mellen Research University Press, 1991). An interesting counterpoint to the state versus society discussion is found in Adrian Jones, *Late, Imperial Russia: An Interpretation: Three Visions, Two Cultures, One Peasantry* (Bern: Peter Lang, 1997).

10. Among the best studies covering one of these areas of civil life are Nancy M. Frieden, *Russian Physicians in an Era of Reform and Revolution, 1856–1905* (Princeton: Princeton University Press, 1981) and Jeffery Brooks, *When Russia Learned to Read: Literacy and Popular Literature, 1861–1917* (Princeton: Princeton University Press, 1985). Despite the restrictions of the Tsarist government, civil society was growing during the final years of the regime.

11. Walkin, *The Rise of Democracy in Pre-Revolutionary Russia*, 121.

12. Porter, *The Zemstvo and the Emergence of Civil Society*, 24–27.

13. Ibid., 44.

14. The best overview of the zemstvo movement is in the essays collected in Terence Emmons and Wayne S. Vucinich, eds *The Zemstvo in Russia: An Experiment in Local Self-Government* (Cambridge: Cambridge University Press, 1982). The comparatively neglected Union of Towns is discussed in William E. Gleason, "The All-Russian Union of Towns and the Politics of Urban Reform in Tsarist Russia" *Russian Review* 35 (July 1976): 290-302.

15. Ruth A. Roosa and Thomas C. Owen, *Russian Industrialists in an Era of Revolution: The Association of Industry and Trade, 1906–1917* (Armonk, N.Y.: M. E. Sharpe, 1997), 2–3.

16. Ibid., 6–27

1—The Early War Orders

1. In recent years a number of historians questioned the extent of popular support that the war enjoyed in July 1914. Allan Wildman suggests that, while the enthusiasm of the educated elites was genuine, the peasants making up the

majority of mobilized troops did not share it. Allan K. Wildman, *The End of the Russian Imperial Army,* Vol. 1: *The Old Army and the Soldiers' Revolt (March–April 1917)* (Princeton: Princeton University Press, 1980), 76–80.

2. Raymond Pearson, *The Russian Moderates and the Crisis of Tsarism, 1914–1917* (New York: Barnes and Noble Books, 1977), 20.

3. *Report of the Central Committee of the All-Russian Union of Zemstvos,* 30; quoted in Tikhon Polner, *Russian Local Government During the War and the Union of Zemstvos,* The Carnegie Endowment for International Peace, Division of Economics and History. Russian Series, ed. James T. Shotwell, LL.D. (New Haven: Yale University Press, 1930), 57.

4. Nicholas Golovin, "The Russian War Plan of 1914," *Slavonic and East European Review* 14 (1935–36): 564–68.

5. E. R. Goldstein, "Military Aspects of Russian Industrialization: The Defense Industries, 1890–1917" (Ph.D. diss., Case Western Reserve University, 1971), 182, 185.

6. In the years immediately prior to World War I, the Russian government had embarked on a major artillery rearmament project based on the lessons of the Russo-Japanese War. During the Russo-Japanese War, the 1,276 artillery pieces employed had consumed some 918,000 shells. This figure of almost 720 rounds per gun during the course of the war became the basis of most future calculation. After several years of discussion, the War Ministry established a reserve requirement of one thousand shells per 3 inch gun. While an increase over earlier standards, the thousand-round reserve represented approximately one hundred minutes of sustained fire at the maximum combat rate.

In 1910, a special commission of the General Staff under General Polivanov reconsidered the ammunition reserve issue. The resulting figures were explicitly predicated on the idea that no future war would last more than a year and that ammunition reserves existed solely to fill the gap until industry could commence wartime production. The latter conclusion is particularly astonishing given the committee's awareness of the failure of Russian industry to meet production needs during the Russo-Japanese War.

Lest the Russian failure be considered a unique case, the British Army used its experiences in the Boer War as the basis for its own artillery requirements. The 1905 British standard was five hundred rounds in the field per gun. When the war opened in 1914, the British standard stood at one thousand rounds per gun in the field, with an additional five hundred in reserve in Britain. British war planning also called for sufficient emergency contracts to be let at the outbreak of hostilities to provide an additional five hundred rounds per gun during the following six months. Goldstein, "Military Aspects of Russian Industrialization," 147–52 and 173–80; David French, "The Military Background to the 'Shell Crisis' of May 1915," *Journal of Strategic Studies* 2 (September 1979): 193–94.

7. Goldstein, "Military Aspects of Russian Industrialization," 144–46.

8. During this period, the Russian ruble traded at between 1.5 and 2 rubles to the dollar. J. N. Westwood, *A History of Russian Railways* (London: George Allen and Unwin, 1964), 157–59.

9. Goldstein, "Military Aspects of Russian Industrialization," 82–87.

10. Ibid., 169–70.

11. Lewis H. Siegelbaum, *The Politics of Industrial Mobilization in Russia: A Study of the War-Industries Committees* (New York: St. Martin's Press, 1983), 27.

12. "Memorandum regarding activities of J. P. Morgan and Co. as purchasing agents for the British and French Governments," Folder 773, Box 82, Papers of Edward Reilly Stettinius, Sr. (hereafter Stettinius Papers), Albert H. Small Special Collections Library, University of Virginia; *New York Times*, June 14, 1915.

13. For more on the reliability of this source, see pages 103–4. Moisei I. Gaiduk, *Utiur: Materialy i fakty o zagotovitel'noi deiatel'nosti russkikh voennykh komissii v Amerike* (New York: Russkii Golos, 1918), 10–11.

14. "Memorandum regarding activities of J. P. Morgan and Co. as purchasing agents for the British and French Governments," Folder 773, Box 82, Stettinius Papers.

15. *New York Times*, December 2, 1914.

16. *New York Times*, November 27, 1914.

17. A typical example was carried on Page One under the headline "DISOWNED AS WAR BUYERS—British Embassy Denies Knowledge of Capt. Webb and J. H. Boyd." The purchasing situation was confused enough that the embassy could not be unequivocal in its denunciation, the official text reading "The British Embassy has no knowledge that these gentlemen have authority to purchase on behalf of the British or Canadian Governments." *New York Times*, December 18, 1914.

18. Bryan would not comment on whether the building of submarines in section would be legal, a practice the United States had permitted during the Russo-Japanese War. *New York Times*, December 2, 1914.

19. *New York Times*, May 7, 1915.

20. Kathleen Burk, *Britain, America and the Sinews of War, 1914–1918* (Boston: George Allen and Unwin, 1985), 7.

21. United States, National Archives and Records Administration, National Archives II, College Park, Maryland, Records Group 261, Records of Former Russian Agencies in the United States (hereafter RG 261), Records of the Agent of Trade and Industry, Timacheff, Minister of Commerce, to Medzikhovsky, Western Union Cablegram, August 25, 1914.

22. *Advertiser* (London, Ontario), October 28, 1914; RG 261, Records of the Agent of Trade and Industry, Medzikhovsky to Minister of Commerce, Canadian Pacific Telegraph Cablegram, September 4, 1914.

23. RG 261, Records of the Agent of Trade and Industry, Medzikhovsky to Sir Joseph Pope, Under Secretary of State for External Affairs, Western Union Day Letter, October 7, 1914.

24. RG 261, Records of the Agent of Trade and Industry, Furness, Withy and Company to Medzikhovsky, October 8, 1914.

25. RG 261, Records of the Agent of Trade and Industry, Wimbe to Medzikhovsky, et al., Western Union Night Letter, November 23, 1914.

26. *Eary Grey* was returned to Canada along with the *J. D. Hazen*, a later Canadian transfer, during the Allied occupation of Arkhangel'sk in 1918. *Jane's Fighting Ships of World War One* (Jane's Publishing Company, 1919; reprint, New York: Crown Publishers, 1990), 100.
27. RG 261, Records of the Agent of Trade and Industry, Record of Voyage of *S.S. Lintrose* from St. John's, Nfld., to Arkhangel'sk, Russia.
28. Norman Stone, *The Eastern Front, 1914–1917* (New York: Charles Scribner's Sons, 1975), 157–58.
29. The Canadian Car order is used to good effect to illustrate the overall Russian supply effort in Keith E. Neilson, "Russian Foreign Purchasing in the Great War: A Test Case," *Slavonic and Eastern European Review* 60 (October 1982): 572–90.
30. Stone, *The Eastern Front*, 153.
31. E. Macadam, secretary to Hughes, to Russian ambassador, October 13, 1914; quoted in Neilson, "Russian Foreign Purchasing," 574.
32. Neilson, "Russian Foreign Purchasing in the Great War: A Test Case," 577.
33. Ibid., 580.
34. *New York Times*, April 22, 1915.
35. *New York Times*, April 17, 1915 and May 3, 1915.
36. "Memorandum re Westinghouse Contracts for Russian rifles," May 22, 1919, "Westinghouse" Folder, Box 83, Stettinius Papers.
37. *New York Times*, October 1, 1914.
38. "Memorandum regarding activities of J. P. Morgan and Co. as purchasing agents for the British and French Governments," Folder 773, Box 82, Stettinius Papers.
39. *New York Times*, October 29, 1914.
40. *New York Times*, June 14, 1915.
41. *New York Times*, October 7, 1914.
42. United Kingdom, *History of the Ministry of Munitions*, vol. 2, *General Organization for Munitions Supply*, part VIII, *Inter-Allied Organization* (London: His Majesty's Stationery Office, 1921), 18.
43. Burk, *Britain, America and the Sinews of War*, 44–45.
44. United Kingdom, *History of the Ministry of Munitions*, vol. 2, *General Organization for Munitions Supply*, part VIII, *Inter-Allied Organization*, 6-7.
45. Walter Runciman to Grey, August 29, 1914; quoted in Keith Neilson, *Strategy and Supply: The Anglo-Russian Alliance, 1914–17* (London: Allen and Unwin, 1984), 51–52.
46. D. S. Babichev, "Deiatel'nost' russkogo pravitel'stvennogo komiteta v Londone v gody pervoi mirovoi voiny, (1914–1917)" *Istoricheskie Zapiski* 57 (1956): 276–77.
47. Neilson, *Strategy and Supply*, 66.
48. Gaiduk, *Utiur*, 13.
49. *New York Times*, October 1, 1916.
50. *New York Times*, September 16, 1914.
51. Gaiduk, *Utiur*, 28–9.

52. Ibid., 29.
53. Ibid., 29–30.
54. Daphne Stassin Herzstein, "The Diplomacy of Allied Credit Advanced to Russia in World War I" (Ph.D. diss., New York University, 1972), 61.
55. Neilson, *Strategy and Supply*, 54–56; Herzstein, "The Diplomacy of Allied Credit," 83–92.
56. Herzstein, "The Diplomacy of Allied Credit," 83–92.
57. The extraordinary domestic measures that Britain took to secure its gold supply are described in Henry F. Grady, *British War Finance, 1914–1919* (New York: Columbia University Press, 1927; reprint, New York: AMS Press, 1968), 37–50.
58. Benson Lee Grayson, *Russian–American Relations in World War I* (New York: Frederick Ungar Publishing Company, 1979), 6–12.
59. Ibid., 13.
60. Bryan; quoted in Herzstein, "The Diplomacy of Allied Credit," 65.
61. Ibid.
62. *New York Times*, April 22, 1915.
63. As a point of occasional confusion, Ambassador Iurii Petrovich Bakhmetev is no relation of Boris A. Bakhmeteff, representative of the Central War-Industries Committee and later Provisional Government ambassador to the United States.
64. Memorandum by Lansing of meeting with Wilson; quoted in Herzstein, "The Diplomacy of Allied Credit," 75.
65. Grayson, *Russia–American Relations in World War I* , 30–32.
66. Ibid., 77.
67. Neilson, *Strategy and Supply*, 55.
68. Keith Neilson, *Britain and the Last Tsar: British Policy and Russia, 1894–1917* (Oxford: Clarendon Press, 1995), 351; ibid., 104–5.
69. Herzstein, "The Diplomacy of Allied Credit," 114–15.
70. Neilson, *Strategy and Supply*, 67–68; Burk, *Britain, America and the Sinews of War*, 45–46.
71. Herzstein, "The Diplomacy of Allied Credit," 129–31.
72. John Douglas Forbes, *Stettinius, Sr.: Portrait of a Morgan Partner* (Charlottesville: University Press of Virginia, 1974), 46.
73. B. C. Forbes, "The Biggest Buyer in the World," *The American Magazine* (September 1917): 15.
74. The flood of British orders made Stettinius' commission arrangement so lucrative that Morgan quickly bought him out, making him a partner in the firm effective January 1, 1916. For 1915, his commissions from British orders totaled $500,000. Forbes, *Stettinius, Sr.*, 48–49.
75. *New York Times*, February 4, 1915.
76. Forbes, "The Biggest Buyer in the World," 15.
77. Herzstein, "The Diplomacy of Allied Credit," 131.
78. Ibid., 80.
79. Gaiduk, *Utiur*, 20.

80. Major General Sir Alfred Knox, *With the Russian Armies, 1914–1917: Being Chiefly Extracts from the Diary of a Military Attaché*, vol. 1 (London: Hutchinson and Company, 1921; reprint, New York: Arno Press, 1971), 272–73.
81. *New York Times*, June 18, 1915.
82. *New York Times*, July 3, 1915.
83. Herzstein, "The Diplomacy of Allied Credit," 66.
84. *New York Times*, October 1, 1916.

2—The Crisis Breaks

1. *London Times*, May 14, 1915.
2. R. J. Q. Adams, *Arms and the Wizard: Lloyd George and the Ministry of Munitions, 1915–1916* (College Station: Texas A&M University Press, 1978), 30–35.
3. Maurice Paléologue, *An Ambassador's Memoirs*, fourth ed., trans. F. A. Holt, vol. 1 (New York: George H. Doran Company, 1925), 217.
4. Ibid., 221.
5. Ibid., 221–22.
6. Foreign Ministry to Buchanan, March 1, 1915; quoted in Herzstein, "The Diplomacy of Allied Credit," 142.
7. James T. Shotwell, LL.D., ed., *The Carnegie Endowment for International Peace, Division of Economics and History, Russian Series*, vol. 2, *State Control of Industry in Russia During the War*, by Seman Ospiovich Zagorsky (New Haven: Yale University Press, 1928), 75–6.
8. Knox, *With the Russian Army*, vol. 1, 319–20.
9. Ibid.
10. Norman Stone, author of the best general work in English on the Eastern Front, contends that the Russian military leadership "exaggerated" German artillery superiority as an excuse for their tactical failure, observing that the German artillery superiority in the East was no greater that the artillery superiority enjoyed by the Allies in the West. Regardless, the Russian and Allied perceptions of inferiority drove purchasing decisions. Stone, *The Eastern Front*, 144–47.
11. Miliukov, *Political Memoirs*, 316, and Sir Bernard Pares, *The Fall of the Russian Monarchy: An Examination of the Evidence* (New York: Alfred A. Knopf, 1939; Vintage Books, 1961), 242–43, mention Rodzianko's return from the front, while Pearson, *The Russian Moderates*, 34–35, discusses Efremov.
12. Rodzianko, *The Reign of Rasputin*. (Philpot, 1927), 132; quoted in Pares, *The Fall of the Russian Monarchy*, 243.
13. Zagorsky, *State Control of Industry*, 83–85.
14. Siegelbaum, *Politics of Industrial Mobilization*, 40–49.
15. Lewis H. Siegelbaum, "The Workers' Groups and the War-Industrial Committees: Who Used Whom?" *Russian Review* 39 (April 1980), 154.
16. The point is often lost that the authorization of the Central War-Industries Committee was the signal for the formation of the local committees and

that the entire scheme was not in place until fall 1915. Zagorsky, *State Control of Industry*, 86–91.

17. S. L. Sergeeva, *Voenno-promyshlennye komitety v gody pervoi mirovoi voiny* (Moscow: Moscow State Automobile-Roadway Institute, 1996), 74; Gaiduk, *Utiur*, 62–63.

18. Sukhomlinov would ultimately be tried as a German spy. V. I. Gurko, *Features and Figures of the Past: Government and Opinion in the Reign of Nicholas II*, trans. Laura Matveev. (Stanford, California: Leland Stanford Junior University, 1939; reprint, New York: Russell and Russell, 1970), 554.

19. V. V. Shulgin, *Days of the Russian Revolution: Memoirs from the Right, 1905–1917*, trans. Bruce F. Adams (Sofia, 1925; reprint, Gulf Breeze, Florida: Academic International Press, 1990), 41.

20. Knox, *With the Russian Army*, vol. 1, 273–75.

21. For their part, Vickers blamed their failure to deliver on the usual litany of problems with Russian contracts; failure of the Russians to provide components and guns for testing, confusing specifications and blueprints, and intractable Russian inspectors. Stone, *The Eastern Front*, 150–52.

22. Knox, *With the Russian Army*, vol. 1, 273.

23. Grey removed this section prior to forwarding the memo to the British ambassador in Petrograd. Kitchener to Grey, August 5, 1915, quoted in Neilson, *Strategy and Supply*, 104.

24. Ibid., 273–74.

25. Daniel W. Graf, "Military Rule Behind the Russian Front, 1914–1917: The Political Ramifications," *Jahrbucher für Geschichte Osteuropas* 22 (1974), 390–411.

26. Polivanov; quoted in ibid., 404.

27. Bruce Menning, *Bayonets Before Bullets: The Imperial Russian Army, 1861–1914* (Bloomington: Indiana University Press, 1992), 256.

28. Ibid., 274–76.

29. CIR to the Foreign Office, February 2, 1915; quoted in Herzstein, "The Diplomacy of Allied Credit," 140.

30. United Kingdom, *History of the Ministry of Munitions*, vol. 2, *General Organization for Munitions Supply*, part VIII, *Inter-Allied Organization*, 6–8.

31. United Kingdom, *History of the Ministry of Munitions*, vol. 2, *General Organization for Munitions Supply*, part III, *Munitions Organizations in the United States of America* (London: His Majesty's Stationery Office, 1921), 41; Neilson, *Britain and the Last Tsar*, 352–53; Neilson, *Strategy and Supply*, 101.

32. Colonel Beliaev's uncle is the same General Beliaev whom Paléologue visited seeking details of the Russian munitions shortage. The ambassador called the general "a hard worker and the soul of conscience and honour," and his nephew also seems to have acquitted himself well. Paléologue, *An Ambassador's Memoirs*, vol. 1, 221.

33. Herzstein, "The Diplomacy of Allied Credit," 144–45.

34. United Kingdom, *History of the Ministry of Munitions*, vol. 2, *General Organization for Munitions Supply*, part VIII, *Inter-Allied Organization*, 11–12.

35. United Kingdom, *History of the Ministry of Munitions*, vol. 2, *General Organization for Munitions Supply*, part III, *Munitions Organizations in the United States of America*, 39–40.
36. Ibid., 11.
37. Ibid., 41.
38. Ibid.
39. Ibid., 39.
40. Ibid., 41.
41. United Kingdom, *History of the Ministry of Munitions*, vol. 2, *General Organization for Munitions Supply*, part VIII, *Inter-Allied Organization*, 13–14; Neilson, *Britain and the Last Tsar*, 353; Neilson, *Strategy and Supply*; 103–05.
42. William G. Lyddon, *British War Missions to the United States, 1914–1918* (London: Oxford University Press, 1938): 145 *passim*.
43. Burk, *Britain, America and the Sinews of War*, 61–64.
44. Sir John Bradbury, Joint Permanent Secretary to the Treasury, August 31, 1915; quoted in Neilson, *Strategy and Supply*, 106.
45. Ibid.
46. Ibid., 106–7.
47. As Russian supply efforts were enabled only by great financial machinations, Finance Minister Bark was a critical, if distant, figure for the Russian Supply Commission in America. Bark was an industrialist and had served as a member of the council of the Association of Industry and Trade. Roosa and Owen, *Russian Industrialists in an Era of Revolution*, 146.
48. Ibid., 111–12.
49. Ibid., 112–14; Herzstein, "The Diplomacy of Allied Credit," 159–62.
50. Neilson, *Strategy and Supply*, 113; Herzstein, "The Diplomacy of Allied Credit," 162; Siegelbaum, *The Politics of Industrial Mobilization in Russia*, 130.
51. Herzstein, "The Diplomacy of Allied Credit," 147.
52. Ibid., 146.
53. Ibid., 152
54. "Osobyi zhurnal Soveta ministrov," November 3 (Old Style), 1915; quoted in Siegelbaum, *The Politics of Industrial Mobilization in Russia*, 131.
55. Ibid.

3—A Committee in Earnest

1. Letter, Ellershaw to Stettinius, November 11, 1915, Folder 330, Box 20, Stettinius Papers.
2. RG 261, Records of the Office of the Chairman, Minutes of the Meetings of the Russian Supply Committee, "Protokol' pervago zasedaniia Russkago Zagotovitel'nago Komiteta v Amerike ot' 13 Oktiabr' 1915."
3. *New York Times*, July 22, 1951.
4. RG 261, Records of the Office of the Chairman, Minutes of the Meetings

of the Russian Supply Committee, "Protokol' pervago zasedaniia Russkago Zagotovitel'nago Komiteta v Amerike ot' 13 Oktiabr' 1915."

5. Siegelbaum, *The Politics of Industrial Mobilization*, 70–77; Paul P. Gronsky, "The War and the Central Government" in *The War and the Russian Government*, ed. Paul Vinogradoff (New Haven: Yale University Press, 1929), 32–42.

6. RG 261, Records of the Office of the Chairman, "Polozhenie o komitete po zagotovleniiu v Amerike predmetob' boevogo i material'nago snabzheniia apmii."

7. RG 261, Records of the Office of the Chairman, Minutes of the Meetings of the Russian Supply Committee, "Protokol' vtornago zasedaniia Russkago Zagotovitel'nago Komiteta v Amerike ot' 21 Oktiabr' 1915."

8. Ibid.

9. *New York Times*, August 12, 1917.

10. *New York Times*, November 21, 1915; May 31, 1916; June 17, 1916.

11. Miliukov, *Political Memoirs*, 315.

12. Guchkov, head of the Central War-Industries Committee, was the other unacceptable candidate in the 1913 election. Robert W. Thurston, *Liberal City, Conservative State: Moscow and Russia's Urban Crisis, 1906–1914* (New York: Oxford University Press, 1987), 81.

13. The Duma was, in fact, prorogued as it began to assemble on September 3, before Bark arrived in Britain. Siegelbaum, *The Politics of Industrial Mobilization*, 83.

14. Neilson, *Strategy and Supply*, 129–34.

15. Bradbury to Foreign Office, June 10, 1916; quoted in ibid., 190.

16. Herzstein, "The Diplomacy of Allied Credit," 187.

17. Ibid., 190–91.

18. United Kingdom, *History of the Ministry of Munitions*, vol. 2, *General Organization for Munitions Supply*, part VIII, *Inter-Allied Organization*, 13–14.

19. George Arthur, *Life of Lord Kitchener*, vol. 3 (London: Macmillan and Company, 1920), 349–55; Philip Magnus, *Kitchener: Portrait of an Imperialist* (New York: E. P. Dutton and Company, 1959), 376–79; George H. Cassar, *Kitchener: Architect of Victory* (London: William Kimber, 1977): 472–80.

20. Cable, Lloyd George to Minchin, June 14, 1916, Folder 199B, Box 11, Stettinius Papers.

21. Herzstein, "The Diplomacy of Allied Credit," 222–33.

22. RG 261, Records of the Agent of Trade and Industry, "Memorandum of agreement between the Russian and British governments as to the necessary procedure to be established in order to ensure transport of munitions to Russia," May 5, 1916.

23. Knox, *With the Russian Army*, vol. 1, 355–56.

24. B. J. C. McKercher and Keith E. Neilson, "The Triumph of Unarmed Forces: Sweden and the Allied Blockade of Germany, 1914–1917," *Journal of Strategic Studies* 7 (June 1984): 178–99.

25. Knox, *With the Russian Army*, vol. 1 509–11.

26. RG 261, Records of the Agent of Trade and Industry, "Memorandum of Agreement between the Russian Delegates and … Admiralty," April 18, 1916.

27. RG 261, Records of the Agent of Trade and Industry, "Agreement between

the Russian Government Committee ... and ... the Admiralty in respect of payment for Conveyance of Cargo from the Unites States to the White Sea," Season 1916, August 4, 1916.

28. Cable, Denkstein to C. F. Whigham, June 22, 1916, Folder 199B, Box 11, Stettinius Papers.

29. Ibid.

30. Knox, *With the Russian Army*, vol. 1, 272.

31. "Memorandum regarding activities of J. P. Morgan and Co. as purchasing agents for the British and French Governments," Folder 773, Box 82, Stettinius Papers.

32. Lyddon, 145–62.

33. RG 261, Records of the Office of the Chairman, Perelstrous to Merrick, June 15, 1917.

34. General Minchin to Lloyd George, June 21, 1916; quoted in Neilson, *Strategy and Supply*, 187.

35. Ibid., 189.

36. Cable, Denkstein to Stettinius, June 21, 1916, Folder 199B, Box 11, Stettinius Papers.

37. Ibid.

38. Ibid.

39. Gaiduk, *Utiur*, 52.

40. RG 261, Records of the Office of the Chairman, "Amendments put forward by Lieut. General Zaluboffsky to Mr. Wintour's draft agreement between the British and Russian Governments with respect to the formation of an Anglo-Russian Sub-Committee in connection with the Russian Supply Committee in America."

41. Cable, Denkstein to Stettinius, June 21, 1916, Folder 199B, Box 11, Stettinius Papers.

42. The fact that the British Ministry of Munitions provided confidential information to its chief of inspection via Morgan Company channels emphasizes the intimacy of the relationship. Cable, Stettinius to Denkstein, marked "For C. F. Whigham," June 22, 1916, Folder 199B, Box 11, Stettinius Papers.

43. Ibid.

44. Neilson, *Britain and the Last Tsar*, 255–56.

45. RG 261, Records of the Office of the Chairman, Minutes of the Meetings of the Russian Supply Committee, "Protokol' copok-pervago zasedaniia Russkago Zagotovitel'nago Komiteta v Amerike ot' 19 Iiul' 1915.

4—The Russian-British Axis Cemented

1. RG 261, Records of the Office of the Chairman, "Minutes of the Conference of the Anglo-Russian Sub-Committee of August 17, 1916."

2. RG 261, Records of the Office of the Chairman, "Minutes of the Conference of the Anglo-Russian Sub-Committee of October 3, 1916."

3. After Minchin's death, Stettinius would comment "entirely apart from his brilliant intellect, he was a man of singularly fine character and wore as well as any man I ever knew." Letter, Stettinius to Lefroy, September 14, 1922, Folder 199A, Box 11, Stettinius Papers.

4. RG 261, Records of the Office of the Chairman, "Minutes of the Conference of the Anglo-Russian Sub-Committee of August 4, 1916."

5. Neilson, "Russian Foreign Purchasing," 582–85.

6. One side effect of the ongoing problems with the Canadian Car contract was the reluctance of the Russians to place orders with other Canadian suppliers and the reluctance of Canadian firms to quote orders for the Russians. The British government finally succeeded in placing a major contract for 8-inch shells with a Canadian firm in April 1916, but only after stipulating that only British inspectors would be used. United Kingdom, *History of the Ministry of Munitions*, vol. 2, *General Organization for Munitions Supply*, part IV, *Munitions Organizations in the Canada* (London: His Majesty's Stationery Office, 1921), 41.

7. RG 261, Records of the Office of the Chairman, "Minutes of the Conference of the Anglo-Russian Sub-Committee of August 4, 1916."

8. RG 261, Records of the Office of the Chairman, "Minutes of the Conference of the Anglo-Russian Sub-Committee of August 10, 1916."

9. Ibid.

10. RG 261, Records of the Office of the Chairman, "Minutes of the Conference of the Anglo-Russian Sub-Committee on July 31, 1916."

11. RG 261, Records of the Office of the Chairman, Lieutenant-General Zaluboffsky change of command speech, August 25, 1916.

12. Ibid.

13. Ibid.

14. Ibid.

15. Ibid.

16. Promotional brochure for *The Elements of Crime*, 1927, Box 5, Papers of Boris L. Brasol (hereafter Brasol Papers), Library of Congress, Washington, D. C.

17. English translation of "Methods of Criminal Investigation," Box 58, Brasol Papers.

18. Unsigned legal deposition of Boris L. Brasol, November 1929, Box 5, Brasol Papers.

19. Cable, Minchin to Lloyd George, October 18, 1916, Folder 199B, Box 11, Stettinius Papers.

20. Lyddon, 158.

21. RG 261, Records of the Office of the Chairman, "Minutes of the Conference of the Anglo-Russian Sub-Committee of August 14, 1916."

22. William James, *The Code Breakers of Room 40* (New York: St. Martin's Press, 1956), 95–96.

23. Franz von Rintelen, *Dark Invader: Wartime Reminiscences of a German Naval Intelligence Officer* (New York: Macmillan Company, 1933), 121–31.

24. While divining the true history of any sabotage campaign is, at best,

difficult, the German effort in America during the war is unusually well documented. A number of German communications regarding planned operations were intercepted and decoded by the British government. Retained after the war, they became a central exhibit in an almost two decade-long court battle between the sabotage victims and the German government. The court case also served the unique role of collecting and validating documentary evidence and personal testimony on these secret matters. James, *The Code Breakers of Room 40*, 187–95.

25. Jules Witcover, *Sabotage at Black Tom: Imperial Germany's Secret War in America, 1914–1917* (Chapel Hill, NC: Algonquin Books of Chapel Hill, 1989), 321.

26. While German sabotage was the primary concern, there had been isolated incidents of attacks by American anti-war protesters. On July 2 and 3, 1915, an American protester had planted a bomb in the Senate wing of the Capitol building, then traveled to New York, where he unsuccessfully tried to kill J. Pierpont Morgan. Ibid., 110–12.

27. Time would prove correct the Russian assertion that lax security at the yard had permitted its infiltration. Ibid., 152–70.

28. RG 261, Records of the Office of the Chairman, "Protocol of Special Meeting in Connection with the matter of the loss of 900 cases of Shells ... destroyed during the explosion on Black Tom...," October 30, 1917.

29. Florinsky would later be removed from Russian service for alleged pro-German activities. Witcover, *Sabotage at Black Tom*, 187.

30. Ibid., 184–96.

31. Herzstein, "The Diplomacy of Allied Credit," 256–57.

32. Neilson, *Britain and the Last Tsar*, 356–57; Neilson, *Strategy and Supply*, 210–11.

33. Treasury to Foreign Office, November 30, 1916; quoted in Neilson, *Strategy and Supply*, 212.

34. Memorandum re Westinghouse Contracts for Russian rifles," May 22, 1919, "Westinghouse" Folder, Box 83, Stettinius Papers

5—The Zemsky Buy a Railroad: A Case Study

1. Golovin, "The Russian War Plan of 1914," 567–68.

2. For example, between 1909 and 1913, traffic on Russian railroads increased some 30 percent, while the number of rail cars increased ten percent. Westwood, *A History of Russian Railways*, 156.

3. Aleksiei Aleksieevich Brusilov, *A Soldier's Notebook* (London: Macmillan and Company, 1930; reprint, Westport, Conn: Greenwood Press, 1971), 239.

4. Robert W. Coonrod, "The Fourth Duma and the War: 1914–1917" (Ph.D. diss., Stanford University, 1951), 122.

5. Ulrich Trumpener, *Germany and the Ottoman Empire, 1914–1918* (Princeton: Princeton University Press, 1968), 62; David Fromkin, *A Peace to End All*

Peace: The Fall of the Ottoman Empire and the Creation of the Modern Middle East (New York: Avon Books, 1989), 72.

6. Russian requests for assistance were tempered by a strong desire to minimize British and French influence in Turkey. Control of the straits represented a key Russian war aim, and it was not until March and April 1915, that the Russian foreign minister secured qualified assurances that the Allies would defer to Russian claims after the war. Trumpener, *Germany and the Ottoman Empire*, 141–42.

7. Fromkin, *A Peace to End All Peace*, 119–121.

8. This request was less governmental than it would first appear. Prince Oldenburg was the head of the Russian Red Cross before additionally assuming his wartime government post. Zemstvo medical operations at the fronts were conducted under the flag of the Red Cross and initially Oldenburg attempted to restrict the zemstvos to supporting roles. The Red Cross, conservative and largely apolitical, never fully accepted the newcomers. John F. Hutchinson, *Politics and Public Health in Revolutionary Russia, 1890–1918* (Baltimore: Johns Hopkins University Press, 1990), 111–15.

9. The official report of the union recounted the Zemstvo's involvement in the Caucasus with particular pride. The document, with an introduction by Prince Lvov, was translated into English and published in Britain in 1917 and offers a succinct and useful account of the official Zemstvo attitude towards its work. The desire for recognition of the legitimacy and value of their efforts, both at home and aboard, as well as expansive liberal reform, is evident. General Committee of the Russian Union of Zemstvos, *Russian Union of Zemstvos: A Brief Report of the Union's Activities During the War with an Introductory Note by Prince G. E. Lvov* (Moscow, January 1916. Reprint ed. London: London Committee of the Russian Union of Zemstvos, 1917), 2.

10. An excellent overview of the issues involved in the extension of zemstvo authority is found in Mark George, "Liberal Opposition in Wartime Russia: A Case Study of the Town and Zemstvo Unions, 1914–1917," *Slavonic and East European Review* 65 (July 1987): 371–90. Prince Lvov himself typified the zemstvo tendency to assume as much responsibility as others would tolerate. A contemporary recounted a zemstvo meeting which had become occupied with a minor issue. Excusing himself, Lvov left the meeting and organized the purchase of some six millions rubles in factories by phone. When the meeting adjourned and the union treasurer was told of the new arrangement, the treasurer objected to the lack of formal committee authorization. Lvov replied, "We will fill out the forms afterward. The transaction has been settled." Tikhon Polner, *Zhiznennyi put' kniazia Georgiia Evgen'evicha L'vova* (Paris, 1932), 188; quoted in Thomas Fallows, "Politics and the War Effort in Russia: The Union of Zemstvos and the Organization of the Food Supply, 1914–1916," *Slavic Review* 37 (March 1978): 70.

11. General Committee of the Russian Union of Zemstvos, *Russian Union of Zemstvos: A Brief Report*, 31–34.

12. Ibid. 13.

13. W. E. D. Allen and Paul Muratoff, *Caucasian Battlefields: A History of the Wars on the Turco- Caucasian Border, 1828–1921* (Cambridge: Cambridge University Press, 1953): 363–4; Girard L. McEntee, *Military History of the World War* (New York: Charles Scribner's Sons, 1937), 327–29.

14. RG 261, Records of the Pekosnarm (Commission in U.S. of War Supply Committee of Petrograd District), Astroff to General F. F. Minchin, Inspector General, October 20, 1916.

15. David R. Francis, *Dollars and Diplomacy: Ambassador David Rowland Francis and the Fall of Tsarism, 1916–17*, ed. Jamie H. Cockfield (Durham: Duke University Press, 1981), 23.

16. It is a strong commentary on the zemstvo position with both the London and American supply committees that it would be eligible to request and receive these official funds from the British government. None of the correspondence on the order presents this order as a particularly unusual case. For a detailed discussion of the civil representation on the Supply Commission, see pp. 50–51 above. RG 261, Records of the Pekosnarm (Commission in U.S. of War Supply Committee of Petrograd District), Astroff to Minchin, October 20, 1916.

17. N. G. Korsun, *Perevaia mirovaia voina na Kavkazskom fronte* (Moscow: Ministry of Defense of the USSR, 1946), 56.

18. Coonrod, "The Fourth Duma and the War," 122.

19. Norman E. Saul, *Concord and Conflict: The United States and Russia, 1867–1914* (Lawrence: University Press of Kansas, 1996), 409.

20. Westwood, *A History of Russian Railways*, 157–59.

21. O. M. Kerr, *Illustrated Treasury of the American Locomotive Company* (New York: W. W. Norton and Company, 1990), 1–24 *passim*.

22. RG 261, Records of the Agent of Trade and Industry, E. V. Douglas, Secretary of the American Manufactures Export Association, to C. J. Medzikhovsky, October 7, 1914.

23. *New York Times*, April 17, 1915.

24. The exact title of the zemstvo representatives in the United States caused some difficulty for their American contemporaries as well as this study. Most wartime zemstvo activity was, in fact, Zemgor activity, though there is no record of representatives of the All-Russian Union of Towns being in America during this time. The existent records refer to the American Locomotive Company order passing through the "Petrograd Committee for the Supply of the Army" or Pekosnarm. The same representatives and inspectors will refer to themselves as zemstvo and Pekosnarm personnel in contemporary documents.

25. RG 261, Records of the Pekosnarm (Commission in U.S. of War Supply Committee of Petrograd District), Charles M. Muchnic, Vice President of the American Locomotive Company, to the American Commission of All-Russian Zemsky Union, April 19, 1916.

26. RG 261, Records of the Pekosnarm (Commission in U.S. of War Supply Committee of Petrograd District), Charles M. Muchnic, Vice President of the American Locomotive Company, to the American Commission of All-Russian Zemsky Union, April 26, 1916.

27. RG 261, Gololoboff to Pekosnarm, Western Union Cablegram, July 11, 1916.

28. RG 261, Records of the Pekosnarm (Commission in U.S. of War Supply Committee of Petrograd District), Muchnic to Gololoboff, August 11, 1916.

29. RG 261, Gololoboff to Pekosnarm, Western Union Cablegram, August 23, 1916.

30. RG 261, Records of the Pekosnarm (Commission in U.S. of War Supply Committee of Petrograd District), Muchnic to Gololoboff, J. P. Morgan & Company to Ministry of Munitions, hand copy of telegram, August 11, 1916.

31. RG 261, Records of the Pekosnarm (Commission in U.S. of War Supply Committee of Petrograd District), Export Department, J. P. Morgan & Company to Ministry of Munitions, hand copy of telegram, August 25, 1916.

32. RG 261, Astroff to Hermonious, Western Union Cablegram, August 25, 1916.

33. RG 261, Records of the Pekosnarm (Commission in U.S. of War Supply Committee of Petrograd District), Memorandum, Export Department, J. P. Morgan & Company, September 5, 1916.

34. For a detailed discussion of the transportation problem, see pp. 55–56 above.

35. RG 261, Records of the Pekosnarm (Commission in U.S. of War Supply Committee of Petrograd District), C. J. Medzikhovsky to Charles M. Muchnic, vice president of the American Locomotive Company, July 28, 1916.

36. RG 261, Records of the Pekosnarm (Commission in U.S. of War Supply Committee of Petrograd District), Muchnic to Professor Michel Gololoboff, August 2, 1916.

37. RG 261, Records of the Pekosnarm (Commission in U.S. of War Supply Committee of Petrograd District), Muchnic to Gololoboff, August 31, 1916; RG 261, Records of the Pekosnarm (Commission in U.S. of War Supply Committee of Petrograd District), N. Vasiloff, et al. to the American Locomotive Company, September 9, 1916; RG 261, Records of the Pekosnarm (Commission in U.S. of War Supply Committee of Petrograd District), E. C. Fisher to Muchnic, October 18, 1916.

38. RG 261, Records of the Pekosnarm (Commission in U.S. of War Supply Committee of Petrograd District), E. C. Fisher, manager, Cooke Works, American Locomotive Company, to Muchnic, October 18, 1916.

39. RG 261, Records of the Pekosnarm (Commission in U.S. of War Supply Committee of Petrograd District), Muchnic to All Russian Zemske [*sic*] Union, October 24, 1916.

40. RG 261, Saknovsky, Poliakoff and Vassilieff to Pekosnarm, Western Union Cablegram, October 24, 1916.

41. This tendency toward group decision making and diffused authority is a common theme throughout Russian war supply efforts both at home and abroad, and stands in marked contrast to the authoritarian powers given supply officials in the other Allied nations. When a French supply minister visited Russia in May 1916, one Russian general was so struck by the amount of control the minister

exercised that he remarked "no one in Russia has such power. We are without a leader ... and yet Russia is an autocracy." More succinctly, the Grand Duke Serge told the same minister "you are an autocrat and I am an anarchist!" The same comments could be applied to the Russian Supply Commission. Knox, *With the Russian Army*, vol.2, 418–19.

42. RG 261, Pekosnarm to Gololoboff, Western Union Cablegram, September 6, 1916.

43. RG 261, Meyer, Vasilieff, Radziminsky, Popereff and Kudriavzeff to Pekosnarm, Western Union Cablegram, September 10, 1916.

44. RG 261, Pekosnarm to Astroff, Western Union Cablegram, September 11, 1916; Vasilieff to Pekosnarm, Western Union Cablegram, October 6, 1916.

45. RG 261, Records of the Pekosnarm (Commission in U.S. of War Supply Committee of Petrograd District), Charles M. Muchnic, vice president of the American Locomotive Company, to the General Russian Counties and Towns Union, October 23, 1916; RG 261, Records of the Pekosnarm (Commission in U.S. of War Supply Committee of Petrograd District), N. Vassilieff and M. V. Koudriavzoff to Charles M. Muchnic, vice president of the American Locomotive Company, November 1, 1916.

46. RG 261, Records of the Pekosnarm (Commission in U.S. of War Supply Committee of Petrograd District), Charles M. Muchnic, vice president of the American Locomotive Company, to the General Russian Counties and Towns Union, November 2, 1916.

47. The overall 180% price increase does not reflect a much larger price increase in specific war related commodities. Grady, *British War Finance*, 166.

48. Charles M. Muchnic, vice president of the American Locomotive Company, to Professor A. Astrof, General Russian Counties and Towns Union, December 28, 1916; Records of the Pekosnarm (Commission in U.S. of War Supply Committee of Petrograd District), RG 261; NARA.

49. RG 261, Records of the Pekosnarm (Commission in U.S. of War Supply Committee of Petrograd District), Charles M. Muchnic, vice president of the American Locomotive Company, to A. Sakhnovsky and N. Vasilieff, January 16, 1917.

50. RG 261, Records of the Pekosnarm (Commission in U.S. of War Supply Committee of Petrograd District), N. Vasilieff and R. Polianoff to Charles M. Muchnic, vice president of the American Locomotive Company, February 13, 1917.

51. RG 261, Vasilieff to Muchnic, April 6, 1917.

52. The Council on National Defense was established by Congress as an industrial advisory board in 1916. After the American declaration of war, the council assumed sweeping powers over industry and trade. It was folded into it's successor organization, the War Industries Board. Bernard M. Baruch, *American Industry in the War: A Report of the War Industries Board* (New York: Prentice-Hall, 1941), 17–19.

53. RG 261, Records of the Pekosnarm (Commission in U.S. of War Supply Committee of Petrograd District), Kapoustine and Vassilieff to Baruch, May 26, 1917.

54. RG 261, Records of the Pekosnarm (Commission in U.S. of War Supply Committee of Petrograd District), Contract between Pekosnarm and American Locomotive, July 9, 1917.

55. RG 261, Records of the Pekosnarm (Commission in U.S. of War Supply Committee of Petrograd District), Muchnic to Kapustine, February 1, 1918.

56. RG 261, Records of the Pekosnarm (Commission in U.S. of War Supply Committee of Petrograd District), Muchnic to Vasilieff, August 15, 1917.

57. RG 261, Records of the Pekosnarm (Commission in U.S. of War Supply Committee of Petrograd District), Muchnic to Vasilieff, October 2, 1917.

58. RG 261, Records of the Pekosnarm (Commission in U.S. of War Supply Committee of Petrograd District), Kapaustine to Muchnic, June 18, 1918.

59. RG 261, Records of the Pekosnarm (Commission in U.S. of War Supply Committee of Petrograd District), Muchnic to S. M. Vauclain, Chairman of the Committee on Production, Council of National Defense, April 22, 1918; RG 261, Records of the Pekosnarm (Commission in U.S. of War Supply Committee of Petrograd District), James Carr, Business Manager, War Industries Board to S. Ughet, Director of Supplies, Russian Supply Commission, June 6, 1918; RG 261, Records of the Pekosnarm (Commission in U.S. of War Supply Committee of Petrograd District), Colonel M. C. Tyler, Director of Military Railways to Director of Supplies, Russian Supply Commission, August 6, 1918.

60. Eugene L. Huddleston, "Uncle Sam's Locomotives: The Legacy of the Controversial USRA," *Trains* 51 (March 1991): 30–38.

61. 2-10-0 is shorthand for the engine's wheel arrangement. Always given in at least three parts, the middle numbers represent the number of drive wheels and thus the engine's power.

62. William D. Edson, "The Russian Decapods," *Railway and Locomotive Historical Society Bulletin* (1971): 64–69.

63. Martin Gilbert, *The First World War: A Complete History*, (New York: Henry Holt and Company, 1994), 401–02.

64. RG 261, Records of the Pekosnarm (Commission in U.S. of War Supply Committee of Petrograd District), Unsigned letter to E. C. Fisher, American Locomotive Plant Manager, Chester, Pa. September 27, 1918

6—The Liberals in Control

1. The most common view that the Allies lost confidence in the Russian war effort after July 1917 is presented in L. P. Morris, "The Russians, the Allies and the War, February–July 1917" *Slavonic and Eastern European Review* 50 (January 1972): 29–48. The case for an earlier and more gradual loss of confidence is found in Keith Neilson, "The Breakup of the Anglo-Russian Alliance: The Question of Supply in 1917." *The International History Review* 3 (January 1981): 62–75.

2. Lvov quoted in Morris, "The Russians, the Allies and the War, February–July 1917": 30.

3. RG 261, "Kopiia kablegrammy na imia voennago agenta v cevero-amerikanckikh soedinennikh shtatakh," March 8/21, 1917.

4. RG 261, Records of the Pekosnarm (Commission in U.S. of War Supply Committee of Petrograd District), Pekosnarm to Vasilieff, no date (approximately March 22, 1917 by context).

5. RG 261, Records of the Pekosnarm (Commission in U.S. of War Supply Committee of Petrograd District), American Commission of the Pekosnarm to Pekosnarm, March 24, 1917.

6. *Foreign Relations of the United States, 1917*: Secretary of State to Ambassdor Francis, March 20, 1917; Ambassador Francis to the Secretary of State, March 20, 1917.

7. *New York Times*, May 30, 1917.

8. *New York Times*, July 7, 1917.

9. *New York Times*, June 20, 1917.

10. *New York Times*, June 9, 1917.

11. *New York Times*, August 12, 1917.

12. *Foreign Relations of the United States, 1918, Russia, vol. 1*: Secretary of Embassy, temporarily in the United States, to the Secretary of State, June 15, 1917.

13. Gaiuk, *Utiur*, 84.

14. Anthony Heywood, *Modernizing Lenin's Russia: Economic Reconstruction, Foreign Trade and the Railways* (New York: Cambridge University Press, 1999): 38–9.

15. *Foreign Relations of the United States, 1918, Russia, vol. 3*: The Secretary of State to the Ambassador in Russia, April 3, 1917.

16. *Foreign Relations of the United States, 1918, Russia, vol. 3*: Ambassador to Russia to the Secretary of State, April 6, 1917.

17. *Foreign Relations of the United States, 1918, Russia, vol. 3*: Ambassador to Russia to the Secretary of State, April 20, 1917.

18. *Foreign Relations of the United States, 1918, Russia, vol. 3*: Ambassador to Russia to the Secretary of State, April 25, 1917.

19. *Foreign Relations of the United States, 1918, Russia, vol. 3*: Secretary of State to the Ambassador to Russia, April 28, 1917.

20. RG 261, Records of the Agent of Trade and Industry, "Memorandum of an arrangement ... by the Secretary of the Treasury ... and the Russian Ambassador," April 24, 1917.

21. United Kingdom, *History of the Ministry of Munitions*, vol. 2, *General Organization for Munitions Supply*, part III, *Munitions Organization in the United States of America*, 121–22.

22. Ibid., 68.

23. RG 261, Records of the Office of the Chairman, "Minutes of the Conference of the Anglo-Russian Sub-Committee of May 3, 1917."

24. RG 261, Records of the Office of the Chairman, "Minutes of the Conference of the Anglo-Russian Sub-Committee of June 11, 1917."

25. *Foreign Relations of the United States, 1918, Russia, vol. 3*: Ambassador to Russia to the Secretary of State, July 17, 1917.

26. *Foreign Relations of the United States, 1918, Russia, vol. 3*: Ambassador to Russia to the Secretary of State, July 22, 1917.

27. *Foreign Relations of the United States, 1918, Russia, vol. 3*: Ambassador to Russia to the Secretary of State, August 2, 1917.

28. Colville Adrian de Rune Barclay to Robert Lansing, July 1, 1917, Arthur Link, ed., *The Papers of Woodrow Wilson, 1917*, (hereafter *PWW*), 43: 67–9.

29. Edward M. House to Wilson, July 23, 1917, *PWW, 1917*, 43: 248–9.

30. *Foreign Relations of the United States, 1918, Russia, vol. 3*: The British Ambassador to the Secretary of State, August 3, 1917.

31. *New York Tribune*, October 16, 1917.

32. *New York Tribune*, October 17, 1917.

33. Russia had ceased legal liquor production at the beginning of the war, and the illicit importation of spirits would likely have been extremely lucrative. *New York Tribune*, October 18, 1917.

34. RG 261, Records of the Agent of Trade and Industry, Lieutenant Francis B. Kirby, R.A. to the Russian Transportation Committee, May 17, 1917.

35. RG 261, Records of the Agent of Trade and Industry, S. S. Flynn, Assistant Operative, U.S. Secret Service, to Medzikhovsky, August 6, 1917.

36. RG 261, Records of the Agent of Trade and Industry, Medzikhovsky to Department of State, "Suggested letter," October 17, 1917

7—Bolshevik Revolution and Closure

1. *Foreign Relations of the United States, 1918, Russia, vol. 1*: Report of the Special Diplomatic Mission to the Secretary of State, August, 1917.

2. *Foreign Relations of the United States, 1918, Russia, vol. 3*: The Special Representative to the Secretary of State, November 24, 1917.

3. United Kingdom, *History of the Ministry of Munitions*, vol. 2, *General Organization for Munitions Supply*, part VIII, *Inter-Allied Organization*, 31.

4. RG 261, Records of the Office of the Chairman, "Minutes of the Conference of the Anglo-Russian Sub-Committee of December 24, 1917."

5. Letter, Lever to Leffingwell, January 20, 1919, "Westinghouse" Folder, Box 83, Stettinius Papers.

6. Memorandum re Westinghouse Contracts for Russian rifles, May 22, 1919, "Westinghouse" Folder, Box 83, Stettinius Papers.

7. *Foreign Relations of the United States, 1918, Russia, vol. 3*: Ambassador to Russia to the Secretary of State, February 8, 1918.

8. *Foreign Relations of the United States, 1918, Russia, vol. 3*: Ambassador to Russia to the Secretary of State, February 12, 1918.

9. *Foreign Relations of the United States, 1918, Russia, vol. 3*: Ambassador to Great Britain to the Secretary of State, February 14, 1918.

10. *Foreign Relations of the United States, 1918, Russia, vol. 3*: Ambassador to Russia to the Secretary of State, February 14, 1918.

11. Lincoln Colcord to Wilson, December 8, 1917, *PWW, 1917–1918*, 45: 251–3.

12. *Foreign Relations of the United States, 1918, Russia, vol. 3*: The assistant secretary of the Treasury to the Counselor for the Department of State, March 5, 1918.

13. RG 261, Records of the Office of the Chairman, "Minutes of the Conference of the Anglo-Russian Sub-Committee of March 15, 1918."

14. RG 261, Pekosnarm to Kapoustine, Pekosnarm Representative in United States, Western Union Cablegram, May 5, 1918.

15. United Kingdom, *History of the Ministry of Munitions*, vol. 2, *General Organization for Munitions Supply*, part VIII, *Inter-Allied Organization*, 32.

16. Anthony Heywood's *Modernizing Lenin's Russia* covers Lomonosov's career in Soviet Russia, ending with his defection to the West in 1927. *New York Times*, June 11, 1918; June 12, 1918; Anthony Heywood, *Modernizing Lenin's Russia*, 45.

17. John A. White, *The Siberian Intervention* (Princeton: Princeton University Press, 1950): 137–8.

18. John Silverlight, *The Victor's Dilemma: Allied Intervention in the Russian Civil War* (New York: Weybright and Talley, 1970), 31.

19. George A. Brinkley, *The Volunteer Army and Allied Intervention in South Russia, 1917–1920* (Notre Dame: University of Notre Dame Press, 1966), 373–74; David S. Fogelsong, *America's Secret War Against Bolshevism: U.S. Intervention in the Russian Civil War, 1917–1920* (Chapel Hill: University of North Carolina Press, 1995), 70–71.

20. Gaiduk, *Utiur*, 5.

21. Robert A. Karlowich, *We Fall and Rise: Russian-Language Newspapers in New York City, 1889–1914* (Metuchen, N.J.: The Scarecrow Press, 1991), 149.

22. RG 261, Records of the Agent of Trade and Industry, L. A. Martens to Bakhmeteff, no date (forwarded with letter dated April 14, 1919).

23. *Foreign Relations of the United States, 1919, Russia*: Acting Secretary to the Commission to Negotiate Peace, March 25, 1919.

24. Ibid. At the time the State Department was forwarding Martens' demands to the Secretary of State at the Paris Peace Conference, the recognized ambassador, Professor Bakhmeteff, was himself at the conference. Bakhmeteff had received American permission to expend the $100,000 to send himself and a Russian delegation and was well received as he solicited support for the White cause. Fogelsong, *America's Secret War Against Bolshevism*, 68–69.

25. *Foreign Relations of the United States, 1919, Russia*: Acting Secretary to the Commission to Negotiate Peace, April 15, 1919.

26. RG 261, Records of the Agent of Trade and Industry, Marten to Coudert Brothers, April 14, 1919.

27. RG 261, Records of the Agent of Trade and Industry, Frank L. Polk, Acting Secretary of State, to Coudert Brothers, April 19, 1919.

28. *Foreign Relations of the United States, 1919, Russia*: Mr. J. H. Fulton of

the National City Bank of New York to the Acting Secretary of State, April 20, 1919.

29. *Foreign Relations of the United States, 1919, Russia*: The Acting Secretary of State to National City Bank of New York, June 24, 1919.

30. *Foreign Relations of the United States, 1919, Russia*: Memorandum by Mr. Basil Miles, in Charge of Russian Affairs, Division of Near Eastern Affairs, Department of State, June 24, 1919.

31. *Foreign Relations of the United States, 1920, vol. 2*: The Russian Ambassador to the Secretary of State, April 28, 1922.

32. *Foreign Relations of the United States, 1920, vol. 2*: Secretary of State to the Russian Ambassador, April 29, 1922.

33. *New York Times*, July 22, 1951,

34. Unsigned legal deposition of Boris L. Brasol, November 1929, Box 5, Brasol Papers.

35. Letter, Brasol to J. T. Harahan, September 4, 1919, Box 17, Brasol Papers.

36. Boris L. Brasol, *Socialism vs. Civilization*. Introduction by T. N. Carver. (New York: Charles Scribner's Sons, 1920); *The World at the Cross Roads* (Boston: Small, Maynard & Company, 1921); *The Balance Sheet of Sovietism* (New York: Duffield and Company, 1922).

37. Letter, Brasol to Breckenridge Long, October 1, 1919, Box 18, Brasol Papers.

38. For examples, see Norman Hapgood, "The Inside Story of Henry Ford's Jew-mania," *Hearst's International* (June and July 1922); John R. Carlson, "Inside the America First movement," *The American Mercury*, January 1942; *New York Evening Journal,* February through March 1921.

39. If not the translator, Brasol clearly distributed the *Protocols of the Elders of Zion* to an American audience. In 1927, one correspondent wrote Brasol that he had "just received the Protocols and am very much obliged to you for them.... [They are] very necessary to one who wants to fully understand the tricks and the tactics of organized Jewry." Letter, W. H. Allen to Brasol, July 26, 1927, Box 16, Brasol Papers.

40. *New York Evening World*, January 13–15, 1933; *New York Post*, January 13, 1933; *New York Times*, January 14–15, 1933.

41. Forbes, *Stettinius, Sr.*, 196–97

8—Conclusion

1 . Zagorsky, *State Control of Industry*, 88.

2 . *Report of the Central Committee of the All-Russian Union of Zemstvos*, nos. 35–36, 25–6; quoted in Fallows, 82.

3 . From Miliukov's "Stupidity or Treason" Speech to the Duma, November 1, 1916, from Gosudarstvennia Duma, chetvertyi sozyv, *Stenograficheskie otchty, Sessiia 5* (Petrograd: Gosudarstvennaia Tipografiia, 1917), 36–37 and 46–48; quoted in George Vernadsky, et al, ed., *A Source Book for Russian History from*

Early Times to 1917, vol. 3, *Alexander II to the February Revolution* (New Haven: Yale University Press, 1972), 870.

4. Miliukov, *Political Memoirs*, 378.

5. Boris A. Bakhmeteff, *The Legacy of War—Peace* (New York: Houghton Mifflin Company, 1927), 7.

6. Ibid., 52.

Bibliography

Archival and Manuscript Sources

Library of Congress. Papers of Boris L. Brasol.
National Archives and Records Administration, College Park, Maryland. Records Group 261, Records of Former Russian Agencies in the United States.
University of Virginia, Albert H. Small Special Collections Library. Papers of Edward Reilly Stettinius, Sr.

Primary Sources

Advertiser (London, Ontario). October 28, 1914.
Bakhmeteff, Boris A. *War and Finance in Russia*. Philadelphia, 1918.
_____. The Legacy of War–Peace. New York: Houghton Mifflon Company, 1927.
Baruch, Bernard M. *American Industry in the War: A Report of the War Industries Board*. New York: Prentice-Hall, 1941.
Brusilov, Aleksiei Aleksieevich. *A Soldier's Notebook*. London: Macmillan and Company, 1930. Reprint, Westport, Conn.: Greenwood Press, 1971.
Francis, David R. *Dollars and Diplomacy: Ambassador David Rowland Francis and the Fall of Tsarism, 1916–17*. Edited by Jamie H. Cockfield. Durham: Duke University Press, 1981.

Gaiduk, Moisei I. *Utiur: Materialy i fakty o zagotovitel'noi deiatel'nosti russkikh voennykh komissii v Amerike.* New York: Russkii Golos, 1918.

General Committee of the Russian Union of Zemstvos. *Russian Union of Zemstvos: A Brief Report of the Union's Activities During the War with an Introductory Note by Prince G. E. Lvov.* Moscow, January 1916. Reprint ed. London: London Committee of the Russian Union of Zemstvos, 1917.

Gurko, V. I. *Features and Figures of the Past: Government and Opinion in the Reign of Nicholas II.* Translated by Laura Matveev. Stanford, CA: Leland Stanford Junior University, 1939. Reprint, New York: Russell and Russell, 1970.

Knox, Major General Sir Alfred. *With the Russian Army, 1914–1917: Being Chiefly Extracts from the Diary of a Military Attaché.* 2 vol. London: Hutchinson and Company, 1921. Reprint, New York: Arno Press, 1971.

Link, Arthur, ed. *The Papers of Woodrow Wilson.* 35 vols. Princeton: Princeton University Press, 1966– .

London Times. May 14, 1915.

Miliukov, Paul. *Political Memoirs, 1905–1917.* Translated by Carl Goldberg. Ann Arbor: University of Michigan Press, 1967.

_____. *Russia and its Crisis.* Reprint, New York: Collier Books, 1962.

New York Times. August 1914–December 1918.

New York Tribune. October 16–18, 1917.

Paléologue, Maurice. *An Ambassador's Memoirs*, fourth edition. Translated by F. A. Holt. 3 vols. New York: George H. Doran Company, 1925.

Pares, Sir Bernard. *The Fall of the Russian Monarchy: An Examination of the Evidence.* New York: Alfred A. Knopf, 1939; Vintage Books, 1961.

Rintelen, Franz von. *Dark Invader: Wartime Reminiscences of a German Naval Intelligence Officer.* New York: Macmillan Company, 1933.

Shulgin, V. V. *Days of the Russian Revolution: Memoirs from the Right, 1905–1917.* Translated by Bruce F. Adams. Sofia, 1925. Reprint, Gulf Breeze, Fla.: Academic International Press, 1990.

United States. Department of State. *Papers Relating to the Foreign Relations of the United States, 1917.* Washington, D.C.: U.S. Government Printing Office, 1926.

_____. *Papers Relating to the Foreign Relations of the United States, 1918, Russia.* 3 vols. Washington, D.C.: U.S. Government Printing Office, 1931.

_____. *Papers Relating to the Foreign Relations of the United States, 1919, Russia.* Washington, D.C.: U.S. Government Printing Office, 1927.

_____. *Papers Relating to the Foreign Relations of the United States, 1920.* 2 vols. Washington, D.C.: U.S. Government Printing Office, 1938.

Secondary Sources

Adams, R. J. Q. *Arms and the Wizard: Lloyd George and the Ministry of Munitions, 1915–1916.* College Station: Texas A&M University Press, 1978.

Allen, W. E. D. and Paul Muratoff. *Caucasian Battlefields: A History of the Wars on the Turco-Caucasian Border, 1828–1921.* Cambridge: Cambridge University Press, 1953.

Arthur, George. *Life of Lord Kitchener.* 3 vols. London: Macmillan and Company, 1920.

Brinkley, George A. *The Volunteer Army and Allied Intervention in South Russia, 1917–1920.* Notre Dame: University of Notre Dame Press, 1966.

Brooks, Jeffrey. *When Russia Learned to Read: Literacy and Popular Literature, 1861–1917.* Princeton: Princeton University Press, 1985.

Burk, Kathleen. *Britain, America and the Sinews of War, 1914–1918.* Boston: George Allen and Unwin, 1985.

Cassar, George H. *Kitchener: Architect of Victory.* London: William Kimber, 1977.

Conroy, Mary Schaeffer, ed. *Emerging Democracy in Late Imperial Russia: Case Studies on Local Self-Government (The Zemstvos), State Duma Elections, the Tsarist Government and the State Council before and during World War I.* Niwot: University Press of Colorado, 1998.

Coonrod, Robert W. "The Fourth Duma and the War, 1914-1917," Ph.D diss., Stanford University, 1951.

Crisp, Olga. *Studies in the Russian Economy Before 1914.* New York: Barnes and Noble Books, 1976.

Emmons, Terence and Wayne S. Vucinich, eds. *The Zemstvo in Russia: An Experiment in Local Self-Government.* Cambridge: Cambridge University Press, 1982.

Fogelsong, David S. *America's Secret War Against Bolshevism: U.S. Intervention in the Russian Civil War, 1917–1920.* Chapel Hill: University of North Carolina Press, 1995.

Forbes, John Douglas. *Stettinius, Sr.: Portrait of a Morgan Partner.* Charlottesville: University Press of Virginia, 1974.

Frieden, Nancy M. *Russian Physicians in an Era of Reform and Revolution, 1856–1905.* Princeton: Princeton University Press, 1981.

Fromkin, David. *A Peace to End All Peace: The Fall of the Ottoman Empire and the Creation of the Modern Middle East.* New York: Avon Books, 1989.

Gilbert, Martin. *The First World War: A Complete History.* New York: Henry Holt and Company, 1994.

Gleason, William E. "The All-Russian Union of Zemstvos and World War 1." In Terence Emmons and Wayne S. Vucinich, ed. *The Zemstvo in Russia: An Experiment in Local Self-Government.* Cambridge: Cambridge University Press, 1982, 365–82.

Goldstein, E. R. "Military Aspects of Russian Industrialization: The Defense Industries, 1890–1917," Ph.D. diss., Case Western Reserve University, 1971.

Grady, Henry F. *British War Finance, 1914–1919.* New York: Columbia University Press, 1927. Reprint, New York: AMS Press, 1968.

Grayson, Benson Lee. *Russian-American Relations in World War I.* New York: Frederick Ungar Publishing Company, 1979.

Gronsky, Paul P. "The War and the Central Government." In *The War and the Russian Government,* ed. Paul Vinogradoff. The Carnegie Endowment for

International Peace, Division of Economics and History. Russian Series. James T. Shotwell, LL.D., general ed. New Haven: Yale University Press, 1929.

Heywood, Anthony. *Modernizing Lenin's Russia: Economic Reconstruction, Foreign Trade and the Railways*. New York: Cambridge University Press, 1999.

Herzstein, Daphne Stassin. "The Diplomacy of Allied Credit Advanced to Russia in World War I." Ph.D. diss., New York University, 1972.

Hughes, Michael. *Diplomacy Before the Russian Revolution: Britian, Russian and the Old Diplomacy 1894–1917*, New York: St. Martin's Press, 2000.

Hutchinson, John F. *Politics and Public Health in Revolutionary Russia, 1890–1918*. Baltimore: Johns Hopkins University Press, 1990.

James, William. *The Code Breakers of Room 40*. New York: St. Martin's Press, 1956.

Jane's Fighting Ships of World War One. Jane's Publishing Company, 1919. Reprint, New York: Crown Publishers, 1990.

Jones, Adrian. *Late-Imperial Russia: An Interpretation: Three Visions, Two Cultures, One Peasantry*. Bern: Peter Lang, 1997.

Karlowich, Robert A. *We Fall and Rise: Russian-Language Newspapers in New York City, 1889–1914*. Metuchen, N.J.: The Scarecrow Press, 1991.

Kerr, O. M. *Illustrated Treasury of the American Locomotive Company*. New York: W. W. Norton and Company, 1990.

Korsun, N. G. *Perevaia mirovaia voina na Kavkazskom fronte*. Moscow: Ministry of Defense of the USSR, 1946.

Lyddon, William G. *British War Missions to the United States, 1914–1918*. London: Oxford University Press, 1938.

Magnus, Philip. *Kitchener: Portrait of an Imperialist*. New York: E. P. Dutton and Company, 1959.

McEntee, Girard L. *Military History of the World War*. New York: Charles Scribner's Sons, 1937.

McKean, Robert B. *St. Petersburg Between the Revolutions: Workers and Revolutionaries, June 1907–February 1917*. New Haven: Yale University Press, 1990.

Menning, Bruce. *Bayonets Before Bullets: The Imperial Russian Army, 1861–1914*. Bloomington: Indiana University Press, 1992.

Neilson, Keith E. *Britain and the Last Tsar: British Policy and Russia, 1894–1917*. Oxford: Clarendon Press, 1995.

_____. *Strategy and Supply: The Anglo-Russian Alliance, 1914–17*. London: Allen and Unwin, 1984.

Pearson, Raymond. *The Russian Moderates and the Crisis of Tsarism, 1914–1917*. New York: Barnes and Noble Books, 1977.

Pipes, Richard. *Russia under the Old Regime*. New York: Charles Scribners' Sons, 1974.

Polner, Tikhon. *Russian Local Government During the War and the Union of Zemstvos*. The Carnegie Endowment for International Peace, Division of Economics and History. Russian Series. James T. Shotwell, LL.D., ed. New Haven: Yale University Press, 1930.

Porter, Thomas Earl. *The Zemstvo and the Emergence of Civil Society in Late Impe-*

rial Russia, 1864–1917. Distinguished dissertations series. San Francisco: Mellen Research University Press, 1991.

Robbins, Richard G. *The Tsar's Viceroys: Russian Provincial Governors in the Last Years of the Empire.* Ithaca, N.Y.: Cornell University Press, 1987.

Roosa, Ruth A. and Thomas C. Owen. *Russian Industrialists in an Era of Revolution: The Association of Industry and Trade, 1906–1917.* Armonk, N.Y.: M. E. Sharpe, 1997.

Saul, Norman E. *Concord and Conflict: The United States and Russia, 1867–1914.* Lawrence: University Press of Kansas, 1996.

Sergeeva, S. L. *Voenno-promyshlennye komitety v gody pervoi mirovoi voiny.* Moscow: Moscow State Automobile-Roadway Institute, 1996.

Shotwell, James T., LL.D., ed. *The Carnegie Endowment for International Peace, Division of Economics and History, Russian Series.* Vol. 2, *State Control of Industry in Russia During the War,* by Seman Ospiovich Zagorsky. New Haven: Yale University Press, 1928.

Siegelbaum, Lewis H. *The Politics of Industrial Mobilization in Russia: A Study of the War-Industries Committees.* New York: St. Martin's Press, 1983.

Silverlight, John. *The Victor's Dilemma: Allied Intervention in the Russian Civil War.* New York: Weybright and Talley, 1970.

Stone, Norman. *The Eastern Front, 1914–1917.* New York: Charles Scribner's Sons, 1975.

Thurston, Robert W. *Liberal City, Conservative State: Moscow and Russia's Urban Crisis, 1906–1914.* New York: Oxford University Press, 1987.

Trumpener, Ulrich. *Germany and the Ottoman Empire, 1914–1918.* Princeton: Princeton University Press, 1968.

United Kingdom. *History of the Ministry of Munitions.* 6 vols. London: His Majesty's Stationery Office, 1921–2.

Vernadsky, George, et al, ed. *A Source Book for Russian History from Early Times to 1917,* 3 vol. New Haven: Yale University Press, 1972.

Von Laue, Theodore H. "The Prospects of Liberal Democracy in Tsarist Russia." In *Essays on Russian Liberalism,* ed. Charles E. Timberlake, 164–81. Columbia: University of Missouri Press, 1972.

_____. *Sergei Witte and the Industrialization of Russia.* New York: Atheneum Press, 1969.

Walkin, Jacob. *The Rise of Democracy in Pre-Revolutionary Russia: Political and Social Institutions Under the Last Three Czars.* New York: Fredrick A. Praeger, 1962.

Weber, Eugen. *Peasants into Frenchmen: The Modernization of Rural France, 1870–1914.* Stanford: Stanford University Press, 1976.

Westwood, J. N. *A History of Russian Railways.* London: George Allen and Unwin, 1964.

White, John A. *The Siberian Intervention.* Princeton: Princeton University Press, 1950.

Wildman, Allan K. *The End of the Russian Imperial Army* Vol. 1: *The Old Army and the Soldiers' Revolt (March–April 1917).* Princeton: Princeton University Press, 1980.

Witcover, Jules. *Sabotage at Black Tom: Imperial Germany's Secret War in America, 1914–1917*. Chapel Hill, N.C.: Algonquin Books of Chapel Hill, 1989.

Zagorsky, Seman Ospiovich. *State Control of Industry in Russia During the War*. The Carnegie Endowment for International Peace, Division of Economics and History. Russian Series Vol. 2. James T. Shotwell, LL.D., general ed. New Haven: Yale University Press, 1928.

Journal Articles

Babichev, D. S. "Deiatel'nost' russkogo pravitel'stvennogo komiteta v Londone v gody pervoi mirovoi voiny, (1914–1917)." *Istoricheskie Zapiski* 57 (1956): 276–92.

Cracraft, James. "Empire Versus Nation: Russian Political Theory under Peter I." *Harvard Ukrainian Studies* (December 1986): 524–41.

Edson, William D. "The Russian Decapods." *Railway and Locomotive Historical Society Bulletin* (1971): 64–76.

Fallows, Thomas. "Politics and the War Effort in Russia: The Union of Zemstvos and the Organization of the Food Supply, 1914–1916." *Slavic Review* 37 (March 1978): 70–90.

Forbes, B. C. "The Biggest Buyer in the World." *The American Magazine* (September 1917): 15.

French, David. "The Military Background to the 'Shell Crisis' of May 1915." *Journal of Strategic Studies* 2 (September 1979): 192–205.

George, Mark. "Liberal Opposition in Wartime Russia: A Case Study of the Town and Zemstvo Unions, 1914–1917." *Slavonic and East European Review* 65 (July 1987): 371–90.

Gleason, William E., "The All-Russian Union of Towns and the Politics of Urban Reform in Tsarist Russia." *Russian Review* 35 (July 1976): 290–302.

Golovin, Nicholas. "The Russian War Plan of 1914." *Slavonic and East European Review* 14 (1935–36): 564–84.

Graf, Daniel W. "Military Rule Behind the Russian Front, 1914–1917: The Political Ramifications." *Jahrbucher für Geschichte Osteuropas* 22 (1974), 390–411.

Huddleston, Eugene L. "Uncle Sam's Locomotives: The Legacy of the Controversial USRA." *Trains* 51 (March 1991): 30–38.

McKercher, B. J. C. and Keith E. Neilson. "'The Triumph of Unarmed Forces: Sweden and the Allied Blockade of Germany, 1914–1917." *Journal of Strategic Studies* 7 (June 1984): 178–99.

Maddox, Robert J. "Woodrow Wilson, the Russian Embassy and Siberian Intervention."
Pacific Historical Review 26 (1967): 435–48.

Morris, L. P. "The Russians, the Allies and the War, February–July 1917." *Slavonic and Eastern European Review* 50 (January 1972): 29–48.

Neilson, Keith E. "The Breakup of the Anglo-Russian Alliance: The Question of Supply in 1917." *The International History Review* 3 (January 1981): 62–75.

_____. "Russian Foreign Purchasing in the Great War: A Test Case." *Slavonic and Eastern European Review* 60 (October 1982): 572–90.

Siegelbaum, Lewis H. "The Workers' Groups and the War-Industrial Committees: Who Used Whom?" *Russian Review* 39 (April 1980): 150–80.

Index

Agafononv, V. V. 16
Alexander III 6
All-Russian Congress of the Association of Industry and Trade 36, 37, 114
All-Russian Union of Towns 12, 49, 50, 90, 121; *see also* Zemgor
All-Russian Union of Zemstvos 12, 49, 50, 77, 87, 90, 113, 121; *see also* Zemgor
Allison, J. Wesley 17
American Locomotive Company 9, 20, 38, 75–86, 92
Anglo-Russian Committee of Supply 23
Anglo-Russian Sub-Committee (of the Russian Supply Commission in America) 60–70, 72, 93, 100, 102, 115, 116, 125–127
Arkhangel'sk 16, 17, 18, 53–56, 80, 81, 83, 85, 95, 96, 103
Association of Industry and Trade (Russia) 8, 36, 37
Astroff, A. I. 69, 81, 82, 83

Bahkmetev, Iurii P. 27
Bakhmeteff, Boris A. 37, 49, 62, 69, 89, 90, 95, 96, 100–102, 104–107, 112, 115, 116
Baldwin Locomotive Company 78, 84, 86
Bark, Peter L. 28, 43–45, 52–54, 91
Baron Driesen (ship) 96
Baruch, Bernard M. 84, 92
Beliaev, Gen. Mikhail A. 34, 40
Beliaev, Col. N. 40, 54, 72
Benkendorf, Alexander 23, 54, 63, 127
Bethlehem Steel Company 38
Black Tom Port Facility, New Jersey explosion at 71, 115
Bolsheviks 3, 12, 99, 102, 103, 105, 106, 115, 116
Borden, Sir Robert 19
Brasol, Boris L. 68–69, 106–108
Brest-Litovsk, Treaty of 86, 116
Brusilov, General Aleksiei A. 76, 115
Bryan, William J. 16, 26, 89
Bureaucracy, Russian 4–5, 14, 78, 91, 109, 110

Canada: Russian purchase of icebreakers

in 17–19; Russian purchasing in 19–20, 39; *see also* Canadian Car and Foundry Company
Canadian Car and Foundry Company 19–20, 65–66, 70, 79, 126; explosion at Kingsland plant 71–72
Catto, T. S. 42
Caucasian Front 76–77
Central War-Industries Committee *see* War-Industries Committees
Chief Artillery Directorate *see Glavnoe Artilleriiskoe Upravlenie*
Chief Technical Directorate *see Glavnoe Tekhnicheskoe Upravlenie*
Civil Society, Russian 2–7, 12, 36–38, 49, 75, 89, 109, 111–112
Colcord, Lincoln 101
Commission Internationale de Ravitaillement (CIR) 23, 40, 42, 44, 48, 102, 113, 117–118
Coudert Brothers 105

Davison, Henry 29
de Routkowsky, Russian Representative 40
Duma, Russian 11, 36, 38, 50, 51, 76, 78, 80, 112, 113, 114, 115

Earl Grey (Icebreaker) 17, 18
Easter Uprising (Ireland) 1916 54
Eddystone Ammunition Corporation 64
Efremov, Duma Deputy 36
Egyptian State Railway: orders delayed by Russian work 81
Ellershaw, Col. Wilfred 38, 40, 42, 47–48, 53–54, 65, 114, 115
Erzerum: Russian capture of 77

Florinsky, Dmitri 71
Francis, David R. 89, 90, 91, 94, 100–101
Furness, Withy and Company 17, 18

Gaiduk, Moisei I. 103–104
Galicia 35–38, 39, 71, 114, 115
Gavrilov, S. I. 37
General Electric 100
George, Lloyd 29, 34, 51, 53, 59, 72
George V 62
Glavnoe Artilleriiskoe Upravlenie (Chief Artillery Directorate) 14, 38–40, 48, 64, 93
Glavnoe Tekhnicheskoe Upravlenie (Chief Technical Directorate) 48, 56
Gold reserves, Russian 25–28, 43–44, 105
Golevskii, Colonel Nikolai 23–24, 31, 48, 69
Gololoboff, Prof. Michel 80–83
Great Britain: finances 25, 27–28, 43–44, 93–95; loans to Russia 25, 27, 44, 95, 115; shell crisis and 33–34
Great Reforms 6
Grey, Edward 54, 62, 63, 127

Hampshire (British cruiser) 53
Hermonius, Gen. E. K. 40, 42, 48, 52, 54, 60, 62, 81, 108, 114
House, Col. Edward 95, 99, 115
Hughes, Charles E. 106
Hughes, Sam 19

Icebreakers 17–19
Ignatiev, Russian War Ministry Representative 28
Inspections and inspectors: British 56–59, 64–65, 69–70; Russian 56–59, 63–65, 126–127
Inter-Allied Munitions Conference (London, 1915) 51–52, 114
Inter-Allied Supply Conference (London, 1916) 72, 115
Ireland, uprising in 54

Japan: Member of *Commission Internationale de Ravitaillement* 23; Russian purchasing in 34, 44
J. L. Horne (Icebreaker) 17, 18
J. P. Morgan and Company 15, 21, 22, 26, 28–30, 41–44, 47, 55–57, 59–61, 64, 66, 81, 94, 102, 108, 114, 115, 118, 120, 126

Kanada (re-named icebreaker *Earl Grey*) 18
Kenyon, Col. R. L. 69, 70
Khrabroff, Gen. 64, 90, 93, 115
Kingsland, New Jersey, munitions factory explosion 71–72, 115
Kirby, Lt. Francis 96
Kitchener, Field Marshal Earl Horatio

H. 19, 28, 38–41, 43, 47, 53, 62, 78, 110, 114, 115
Knox, Gen. Sir Alfred 35, 57
Korf, Baron O. A. 15, 24

Lansing, Robert 26, 27, 91
Lima Locomotive Works 78
Lintrose (Icebreaker) 18
Lomonosov, George 90, 102
Lvov, Prince George E. 12, 50, 51, 77, 87, 88, 111

Mackie, Colonel Herbert 19, 20
Maklakov, Nikolai 51
Martens, Ludwig A. 104–106
McKenna, Reginald 54
Medzikhovsky, Constantine 16–18, 24, 79, 81, 96–97
Meyer, Inspector 82, 83
Miliukov, Paul N. 2n. 1, 12, 38, 87, 89, 112
Minchin, Gen. F. F. 53, 54, 58, 59, 61, 62, 64–65, 69–70, 81, 115
Mobilization (1914) 12–13, 113
Muchnic, Charles M. 79, 80, 81, 82, 83, 84, 85, 86
Murmansk 103

Narodny, Ivan 16
National Association of Manufacturers (United States) 27
National City Bank of New York 27, 105, 106
New England Westinghouse 21; *see also* Westinghouse Electric Company
Nicholas II 6, 7, 12, 36, 50, 114, 115
Nicholas, Grand Duke 34, 36, 38, 40, 53, 110, 114

Okuntsov, Ivan K. 103
Oldenburg, Prince Alexander 76
Omsk (Russian Volunteer Fleet freighter) 82
Oranovski, Col. 90

Paléologue, Georges Maurice 34
Pressed Steel Car Company 20
Provisional Government, Russian 87–89, 104–106
Pullman Car Company 30–31

R. Martins and Company 18
Railroads *see* Russia: foreign orders for railroad equipment, railroads; United States: Railroad Administration, railroad backlog
Red Cross: American 89; Russian 8, *77n.*
Remington Arms 30, 114
Riabouchinsky, Nicholas 51
Riabushinskii, Pavel 37
Rintelen, Franz von 70
Roebling Wire and Cable Company 70
Rodzianko, Mikhail 11, 36
Root Mission 99
Rusin, Adm. A. I. 52
Russia: finances 25–28, 43–44, 105; *see* gold reserves, Russian; foreign orders for artillery shells 13, 14, 20, 38, 39, 41, 65, 70; foreign orders for heavy artillery 72; foreign orders for railroad equipment (locomotives, cars, rails) 13, 16–18, 30–31, 52, 72–73, 75–86, 91–92, 102; foreign orders for raw materials 14; foreign orders for rifles 13–14, 21, 30, 42, 73, 100, 114; foreign purchasing in pre-war Russian planning *131n.6*; loans from Great Britain 25, 27, 44, 95, 115; Ministry of Commerce 16, 17, 18, 72, 79, 110; Ministry of Ways and Communications 49, 52, 78, 89, 90; Provisional Government 87–89, 115; railroads 13, 55–56, 72, 75–78, 95–96, 102; shell crisis 34–36; transportation problems 16, 18, 42, 47–48, 54–56, 72, 79–82, 95–96; *see also* bureaucracy, Russian; civil society, Russian; inspectors and inspections, Russia
Russian Chamber of Commerce (United States) 16
Russian Government Committee in London 18, 23, 44, 48, 49, 55, 67, 80, 81, 102, 114, 116, 117, 118
Russian Supply Commission in London *see* Russian Government Committee in London
Russian Supply Committee in America: composition 48–49; founded 44, 114; statute 119–123; *see also* Anglo-Russian Sub-Committee
Russian Volunteer Fleet 82, 103, 108

Russkii Golos ("The Russian Voice") 103
Russo-Japanese War 7, 14

Sabotage, German 56, 70–71, 96
Sakhnovsky, Alexander 50, 89, 90
Sapojnikov, A. V. 23–24, 42, 48, 49, 50, 55, 59, 60, 62, 66, 69
Sazonov, Sergei 34
Secret Service: British 71, 96; United States 96
Shcherbatskii Commission 14–15, 23
"Shell crisis" (1915) 114; civil society and 36–38; government response 36, 110; military effects 33–36
Sherchenko, K. P. 15, 24
Special Committee *see* Special Councils
"Special Councils" (Russia) 36, 49, 67, 69, 110, 114, 121, 122, 123
Stavka 38, 39, 53, 110
Stettinius, Edward, Sr. 29, 47, 54, 59, 61, 62, 64, 108, 114, *140n.3*
Stock market, American 20–21
Stolypin, Peter 2
Sukhomlinov, Gen. Vladimir A. 34, 38, 39, 68
Sweden: transport of Russian imports through 55

Timchenko-Ruban, General 23
Turgat (Russian Volunteer Fleet freighter) 82
Transportation *see* Russia, transportation problems
Trepov, A. F. 52, 72

Ughet, Serge 101
U. S. Cartridge Company 20
United States: Council of National Defense 84, 86; economy 20–22; enters war 84, 92–93, 115; inflation in 83; neutrality 16, 17, 26–27, 70, 113; railroad backlog 81
United States Railroad Administration (USRA) 86; War Industries Board 84n. 52, 92, 110, 115
Utro Russii ("Russian Morning") 111

Vasilieff, Inspector 83
Vickers 38
Vladivostok 55, 83, 95, 103
Von Laue, Theodore 2

"War brides" 20
"War Brokers" 15, 21, 22, 26, 29
War-Industries Committees 37, 45, 48–51, 69, 89, 90, 111, 121
Westinghouse Electric Company 20, 21, 58–59, 64, 73, 100
White Russians: supplies for 103–104
Wilson, Woodrow 27, 89, 95, 99, 101, 113
Wimbe, Capt. 17–18
Winchester Repeating Arms Company 21, 42
Wintour, U. F. 40, 60
Witte, Sergei 2, 8, 13
Wozniak, Theodore 71

Zagorsky, Seman 35
Zaluboffsky, Lt. Gen. 60, 61, 66–70, 90, 115
Zemgor 12, 76, 77, 78, 79n. 24, 80, 121; *see also* All-Russian Union of Towns; All-Russian Union of Zemstvos
Zemstvo *see* All-Russian Union of Zemstvos
Zemstvo Act (1864) 6